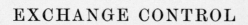

EXCHANGE CONTROL

MACMILLAN AND CO., Limited
LONDON · BOMBAY · CALCUTTA · MADRAS
MELBOURNE

THE MACMILLAN COMPANY
NEW YORK · BOSTON · CHICAGO
DALLAS · ATLANTA · SAN FRANCISCO

THE MACMILLAN COMPANY
OF CANADA, LIMITED
TORONTO

EXCHANGE CONTROL

BY

PAUL EINZIG

MACMILLAN AND CO., LIMITED
ST. MARTIN'S STREET, LONDON
1934

PRINTED IN GREAT BRITAIN
BY R. & R. CLARK, LIMITED, EDINBURGH

32
inzig

CONTENTS

CHAPTER X

CHAPTER XI

CHAPTER XII

CHAPTER XIII

CHAPTER XIV

CHAPTER XV

CHAPTER XVI

CHAPTER XVII

CHAPTER XVIII

PREFACE

EXCHANGE Control is probably the most neglected
section of the science of currency, banking, and
finance. Notwithstanding its great and growing importance, it has practically no literature. While those
who, in the course of their business, have to deal with
exchanges and foreign trade, have to make themselves
acquainted with the rules of Exchange Control as
applied to the particular currencies with which they
are concerned, few of them have realised the significance of the system as a whole. The extent of the prevailing ignorance about Exchange Clearing in particular is really amazing, considering the progress
which that system has made. Very little is known about
it in this country, where no Exchange Clearing agreements operate; but even in countries which have
adopted the system the knowledge acquired in it is
largely one-sided and is confined to the direct experience of the countries in question. Hence the necessity for the publication of a book dealing with Exchange Control in general, and Exchange Clearing in
particular.

Inasmuch as economic literature in the past has
taken notice of Exchange Control at all, it has confined itself to denouncing it and urging its removal.
There has been very little constructive criticism on the
subject. Most economists and financial experts have

carefully abstained from suggesting any improvement of the system for fear that it might be interpreted as an implied recognition of its status. The author's attitude towards Exchange Control is critical but not hostile. He realises the necessity for maintaining the greater part of existing Exchange Control measures so long as general conditions do not improve. He also realises the desirability of retaining some of these measures—such as official intervention in the foreign exchange market—as a permanent part of the monetary system, even after the end of the crisis which brought them into existence. He regards one of them —the system of Exchange Clearing—as the system of the future which will be adopted generally sooner or later as a permanent solution. Many of his critics will probably disagree with him in that respect. Possibly the lesson taught by recent experience will not be sufficient, and another crisis, or several other crises, will be necessary before the world is ripe for the adoption of the obvious solution of its exchange problem.

The author is quite prepared for hostile criticism in the circumstances. He realises that, at the present stage, the line he takes up is not popular, and does not flatter himself by hoping to be able to convert the majority of those who differ from him. He ventures to hope, however, that his effort will increase the interest of experts, and possibly of the public, in this hitherto neglected subject. Whether or not his readers agree with him that Exchange Control is to a great extent a necessary evil, and that a certain part of the system is decidedly desirable, they must take a greater interest in the subject. They may oppose Exchange Clearing, but they cannot afford to ignore it. If this book elicits a widespread discussion of the system, even though the majority of critics will condemn its conclusions, the author will feel that he has attained his end.

P. E.

The White Cottage,
South Bolton Gardens, S.W.5
May 1934

CHAPTER I

INTRODUCTORY

THE two decades which have elapsed between 1914 and 1934 have witnessed a ceaseless struggle between economic freedom and Government intervention in many spheres of economic activity. The principle of *laissez-faire*, the application of which was regarded before the war as the ideal which the world should set itself, has been called in question. The idea of economic planning, which before the war was practically non-existent, has been gaining ground, and in more than one country has been adopted as the guiding principle in the domain of production. The necessity for some form of regulation of production is increasingly advocated. The number of those who have come to believe in the necessity of intervention in the sphere of distribution, in order to adjust consuming capacity to producing capacity, is growing steadily. There is also a strong and increasing tendency in every country to divert consumption into particular channels, and to curtail its former freedom.

Generally speaking, this tendency towards economic planning has not been continuous. During the war there was a high degree of Government intervention which showed itself at its very worst. As a result, after the termination of hostilities, every nation considered it its foremost task to restore economic freedom as soon as possible. During the years of the boom and those of the world crisis, however, it was economic freedom that showed itself at its very worst. There was, as a result, a revulsion of feeling in favour of intervention and economic planning.

In the sphere of foreign exchanges these various phases of development manifested themselves with particular clarity, though their duration was different. During the war Exchange Control was adopted in a variety of forms in most countries, whether belligerent or neutral. A number of them found it necessary to maintain and even to reinforce Exchange Control during the years of currency confusion that followed the war. Between 1919 and 1926, exchanges in the majority of countries were subject to some form of Government control. During the following five years, however, one country after another removed this control, after having relaxed it gradually. Although it cannot be said that freedom in the pre-war sense of the term returned to the international exchange market, considerable progress was made towards attaining that somewhat modified form of freedom which was adopted as the ideal after the war. The crisis of 1931 resulted in the return of the world to Exchange Control, in many ways to an even greater extent than during and after the war.

It may be said that in hardly any sphere of economic activity has intervention been adopted so wholeheartedly as in the matter of foreign exchanges. This intervention has assumed a large variety of forms. Since the war the science and art of Exchange Control have made immense progress. The primitive methods adopted during the war bear the same comparison to the elaborate systems established in many countries during the crisis as the old spinning-wheel does to the machinery of a modern cotton mill.

Economic literature which, in many respects, is well ahead of practical developments, has completely failed to keep pace with the evolution of Exchange Control. Innumerable articles have been published, it is true, by the contemporary Press dealing with individual instances of Exchange Control as and when they arose. These articles, most of which were forgotten in any case almost immediately after they were published, did not attempt to describe or analyse the system of Exchange Control as a whole. In fact most of those dealing with some of the individual measures did not realise that they were confronted with a problem that is a small part of the whole complex of problems aroused by the development of a new system. There was, indeed, no lack of books published during the crisis on the theory and practice of foreign exchanges. Indeed, there has never been before such an immense output of economic literature in general and literature on currency in particular. None of these books, however, have given adequate attention to Exchange Control. Some publications, compiled by international organisations or by banks, rendered useful service by giving summaries of the rules of exchange restrictions adopted in the particular countries. They confined themselves, however, to supplying the facts relating to one particular kind of Exchange Control without analysing, or even classifying, the various methods adopted in different countries.

Apparently the majority of economists, bankers, and business men have not realised that Exchange Control has grown into a system with immense ramification. They all treat it as an irksome nuisance of a temporary character. They protest against it, and denounce it as the cause of most evils, and think that, in showering all the invective of their vocabulary on those responsible for Exchange Control, they have done their duty to themselves and to mankind. Some of the critics denounce Exchange Control as the principal cause of the crisis, while others regard it merely as the inevitable effect of the crisis. Both schools agree that with the return of normal economic conditions Exchange Control will disappear, and the freedom of exchanges will be restored. While one school believes, however, that the crisis cannot come to an end unless and until Exchange Control is abolished, the other believes that Exchange Control can only be abolished when the crisis is over.

Even if we were to accept the popular conception that Exchange Control is essentially temporary, we maintain that it deserves much closer examination than it has received so far. If only a small percentage of the energy spent on denouncing Exchange Control and demanding its immediate removal had been spent upon studying its causes, nature, and effects, the world would undoubtedly be better off for the knowledge acquired. In the absence of a systematic examination based on regular interchange of information regarding the experience of the various countries, each country has to learn at its own expense when establishing its system of Exchange Control, instead of being able to profit from the experience of other countries. This could be remedied by a systematic pooling and distribution of information by some international organisation. Even if Exchange Control is temporary there is no reason why everything should not be done to study and improve its methods so long as it is applied.

A study of the system of Exchange Control brings to light an immense variety of interesting problems.

Volumes could be written about the reasons for the adoption of Exchange Control, about its methods, its working, and its effects. There are innumerable points of interest connected with the technique of Exchange Control, while the economics of Exchange Control provide an immense unexplored field for the academic economist. In examining the reasons for the adoption of Exchange Control, it is necessary first of all to disabuse our minds of a popular misconception. Many of those who denounce exchange restrictions would like us to believe that the whole thing is merely a manifestation of the folly of mankind, and that the reason why there are exchange restrictions to-day, though there were none before 1914, is that our statesmen are more foolish and wicked than pre-war statesmen were. Admittedly, mentality has changed since 1914, and those in responsible positions are now more receptive towards ideas of intervention than they were in the days when *laissez-faire* reigned supreme. This is, however, an effect rather than a cause of the change of conditions. In regard to foreign exchanges, the situation to-day differs in many respects fundamentally from the pre-war situation. There is, in the first place, an increased volume of liquid funds that can be transferred from one country to another, and an increased inclination on the part of the owners of these funds to transfer them at frequent intervals. Another unsettling factor is the increase of speculation in exchanges, speculation which barely existed before the war. A much more important factor is the increased tendency of trade balances to fluctuate. This again is the effect of a set of underlying causes. There is economic nationalism, with its weapons of tariffs and quotas. There is the varying degree in which Socialism affects wage-levels in various countries. There are the sudden strides made in some countries through new technical processes and improved organisation. There is also the difference between the standard of living in the various countries. Another set of causes which, by contributing towards the instability of exchanges, was responsible for the adoption of Exchange Control, was the shortage and maldistribution of gold after the war. It is difficult to say how far all these factors are permanent, but unquestionably, while they exist it will be difficult for any responsible statesman to decide to return to pre-war freedom or even to the post-war freedom that existed in most countries between 1926 and 1931.

The next step is to investigate the nature of Exchange Control. In the broadest sense of the term it covers even the normal measures taken by central banks in the course of their routine work to protect the stability of the exchange. What we are concerned with, however, are abnormal measures adopted for the defence of the exchange. Some of these measures constitute direct interference with the foreign exchange market, while others seek to attain the desired end through influencing foreign trade or foreign loan markets. The technique and economics of Government operations in exchanges raise a large number of problems worth examination. The classification of the immense variety of exchange restriction measures is in itself a difficult but interesting task. Last, but not least, the investigation of the working of Exchange Clearing agreements is well worth undertaking, for it leads us to a hitherto almost entirely unexplored field with immense possibilities.

The effects of Exchange Control deserve more investigation—and, above all, more impartial investigation—than they have received so far. We have all heard a great deal about the unfavourable effects of exchange restrictions upon international trade. Little has been said, however, of their effect upon exchange rates, prices of commodities and securities, wages, the cost of living, international indebtedness, etc. Still less has been said about the effect of Exchange Control, other than exchange restrictions, upon these and other spheres of economic, social, and political life.

The technical aspects of Exchange Control, as distinct from its economic aspects, consist of a large number of highly complicated and specialised problems. They are concerned with the degree of efficiency of the various kinds of control; with the variety of means of evading or resisting it; with the weapons at the disposal of the authorities for overcoming resistance. The working of the system of blocked currencies is complicated in the extreme, and it is a full-time job for any specialist to acquire a thorough knowledge of it. As for the Exchange Clearing system, it has raised a new set of problems of a technical nature, which require solution in order to secure the smooth working of the system. The "black bourses" of various countries, the relations between official and unofficial exchange quotations, and the organisations through which the Exchange Control is worked, add many more to the formidable list of technical problems connected with Exchange Control.

Those who are not interested in all these practical details can hardly afford to ignore the more fundamental economic problems involved. The controversy over Exchange Control can only gain in clarity by the definition of its ultimate object. Is it the defence of the stability of the currency at all costs? Or is it the defence of the reserves of the countries? Or is it a fight against undervaluation or overvaluation of their currencies? Is it directed against fundamental tendencies or merely against day-to-day fluctuations?

The political aspects of Exchange Control are bound to be of interest to many people who think they can afford to ignore both its technical and its economic aspects. Exchange Control has become a factor of importance in international politics. It has been used as a means for exerting political pressure and as a bargaining counter. Its significance in internal politics is beginning to be realised by those who are desirous of establishing new régimes and initiating new experiments, the success of which stands or falls on the extent to which the flight of capital can be prevented. It is the dream of both Socialists and Fascists in various countries to secure complete control over the international movements of funds in the interest of their political and economic plans.

All these considerations make it well worth while to study closely the system of Exchange Control even if we take it for granted that the system is purely temporary. Moreover, it may well be asked whether we can take it for granted that a return to freedom of exchanges is really a question of time. Even if the reply were in the affirmative, it is safe to assume that after a period of freedom the régime of control will be restored as a result of the next economic crisis. There is, to say the least, a possibility that at least part of the measures of Exchange Control adopted during the last few years will be either retained or restored on some future occasion. It is only if we bear this in mind that we can appreciate the true significance of the system of Exchange Control and the necessity of investigating its problems.

CHAPTER II

WHAT IS EXCHANGE CONTROL?

FIRST of all, it is essential to give a precise definition of
the term "Exchange Control". On various occasions it
is used in differing senses, which at times lead to mis-
understanding. The term "Exchange Control" is very
frequently used as a synonym for exchange restrictions. We shall see later that, while exchange restrictions constitute a category of Exchange Control, there
are many other categories besides. In the jargon of
foreign exchange dealers and the financial Press, "Control" indicates exchange operations undertaken by, or
on behalf of, the monetary authorities. When the City
columns state that "the Control was in the market
yesterday" it means that exchanges were bought or
sold on official account for the purpose of influencing
market tendencies. "Control" in that sense does not
indicate all official transactions. It does not include,
for instance, purchases of foreign currencies for War
Debt payments or other external requirements of the
Government. It only includes such official transactions
as have for their sole purpose the creation or counteracting of certain tendencies in the exchange rates. We
shall see later that this type of operation—which we
propose to indicate under the name of "Intervention"
—is again only one of the categories of Exchange
Control.

In our definition "Exchange Control" is every form
of intervention on the part of the monetary authorities

(Government, Central Bank, or special organisation created for that purpose) aiming at interfering with the tendencies affecting exchange rates. In its broadest sense, Exchange Control constitutes part of the normal functions of a Central Bank. It is considered one of the most important duties of a Central Bank to maintain the external stability of the national currency. It is of course often difficult to draw a line between normal and abnormal control. What would have been regarded as abnormal in pre-war practice was adopted as part of the normal routine of Central Banking during the period of post-war stability between 1925 and 1931; and what is still regarded as highly abnormal to-day might become part of the normal functions of Central Banking to-morrow. It is also difficult sometimes to determine whether certain measures taken by the monetary authorities aim solely, or even mainly, at influencing exchanges. While there are a number of direct measures affecting the foreign exchange market, there are also several kinds of indirect measures which aim at influencing exchanges through the intermediary of their effect on some other factors. In the case of the latter it is the intention in the mind of the authorities which determines whether or not the measures may be regarded as Exchange Control. For instance, if a Government introduces quotas on imports it may do so in order to safeguard internal producers—as in the case of British agricultural quotas—in which case the measure cannot be regarded as Exchange Control. It may, on the other hand, be prompted primarily by the desire to safeguard the currency—such was the case of quotas established by the French Government—in which case the measures may safely be classed among those of Exchange Con-

trol, even though they affect internal trade primarily
and the exchanges only at one remove.

Let us deal first of all with the normal measures of
Exchange Control in the broadest sense. Even the
normal function of the gold standard or gold exchange standard implies an official control of the
exchange rate. The system which should satisfy the
adherents of pure *laissez-faire*, if they were consistent
to their doctrines, would be a free inconvertible paper
currency which is allowed to take care of itself. The
limitation of the fluctuations of the exchange through
the purchase and sale of gold, in the case of the gold
standard, or through the purchase and sale of gold
exchanges, in the case of the gold exchange standard,
constitutes, strictly speaking, an action of Exchange
Control. Next to the free inconvertible currency the
automatic gold standard is the system in which
Exchange Control plays the most subordinate part. In
reality, even before the war the gold standard cannot
be said to have been absolutely automatic. In addition
to buying and selling gold at fixed prices the Central
Banks adopted measures aiming, directly or indirectly,
at controlling the exchange rates. Such measures can
be classed under the following headings:

(1) General monetary policy.
(2) Bank rate policy.
(3) Open market policy.
(4) Foreign exchange policy.

Measures of general monetary policy, such as, for
instance, the maintenance of the note circulation
within certain limits, tended to affect the exchanges
through their influence on the price level. The influence
of the bank rate upon exchanges is too well known to
require repetition. It is necessary to point out, however,

that changes in the bank rate do not always aim at affecting exchange rates and do not always constitute an act of Exchange Control. Similarly, open market policy, which may affect exchange rates through its influence upon interest rates, may or may not be an instrument of Exchange Control. The only normal pre-war weapon in the service of the Exchange Control was foreign exchange policy, better known under its German name of *Devisenpolitik*. This consisted of the endeavours of Central Banks to level up seasonal exchange fluctuations by buying up foreign exchange during the export season and selling them to the market during the import season.

In the present book we are not concerned with these normal measures of Exchange Control. They have always been part of the recognised functions of Central Banks and have been adequately dealt with in the vast literature on the subject. We propose to confine ourselves to the examination of Exchange Control in the narrower sense of the term, covering only the so-called abnormal official measures aiming at influencing exchanges. These measures can be divided into two main categories, namely, direct measures and indirect measures. Direct measures are actions and regulations aiming at affecting foreign exchanges directly. Indirect measures are actions and regulations which aim at affecting exchanges through the intermediary of some other sphere of economic activity.

Direct measures can be summarised under four headings:

(1) Intervention.
(2) Exchange restrictions.
(3) Gold policy.
(4) Exchange Clearing.

(1) By intervention we mean foreign exchange operations undertaken by, or on behalf of, the monetary authorities with the object of influencing the exchange rates. Intervention is the most direct and most evident form of Exchange Control. It may be either active or passive. In the case of active intervention the authorities take the initiative in foreign exchange operations, while in the case of passive intervention they wait for the market to take the initiative. Active intervention, again, may be either offensive or defensive, according to whether the authorities take action in order to bring about a change in the exchange rates or in order to prevent market influences from causing an unwanted change in the exchange rates. Passive intervention may assume the form of support, "pegging" the exchange, or the manipulation of forward rates. Support consists of supplying the market with foreign exchanges or with the national currency —whichever is the case—without endeavouring to maintain the exchange rates rigidly fixed. Pegging consists of supplying the market at a rate which is fixed for a more or less prolonged period. Forward exchange manipulation aims at encouraging or discouraging certain types of foreign exchange transactions by influencing the disparity between spot and forward exchanges.

(2) Exchange restrictions are official measures aiming at the limitation or suppression of the freedom of foreign exchange transactions, and thereby at influencing the tendencies of the exchanges. There are five categories of exchange restrictions:

(1) Restrictions on capital movements.
(2) Restrictions on speculation.
(3) Restrictions on external debt payments.

(4) Restrictions on purchases of currencies by importers.

(5) Restrictions on holdings of foreign currencies.

The restrictions on capital movements, in turn, may assume four different forms:

(1) Restrictions on the purchase of foreign exchanges.

(2) Restrictions on the import or export of securities.

(3) Restrictions on the import or export of national or foreign bank-notes.

(4) Restrictions on the export of gold.

Restrictions on speculation in exchanges may assume three different forms:

(1) Restrictions on the purchase of foreign currencies by residents in the country concerned.

(2) Restrictions on operations in spot or forward exchanges on account of foreign residents.

(3) Restrictions on the granting of credits in the national currency to foreign residents.

The restrictions on holdings of foreign currencies may assume two forms:

(1) Measures compelling the surrender of foreign currencies obtained through exports.

(2) Measures compelling the surrender of old balances or securities held abroad.

The restrictions on external debt payments may assume the following forms:

(1) Transfer moratorium, with unrestricted use of the amounts by the creditors within the debtor country.

(2) Restricted use of the blocked amounts for special types of investments or special types of exports.

(3) Complete blocking of the amounts paid in domestic currency.

(4) Compulsory employment of the amounts on blocked accounts.

The restrictions on the purchases of foreign currencies by importers may be classed under three subheadings:

(1) Prohibition of purchase for the import of luxuries, etc.

(2) Delayed issue of permits for purchases.

(3) Fixing of quotas for the allotment of exchange.

(3) Gold policy can be placed in the service of Exchange Control through a departure from the rules of the gold standard. While nominally on a gold standard, Central Banks can manipulate the buying or selling price of gold in such a way as to affect gold points and thereby affect exchange rates. Much more important than this method is the method of controlling exchange by changing the official price of gold.

(4) Exchange Clearing is a measure aiming at controlling the exchanges by obviating the necessity for transfers through the foreign exchange market. As it interferes with the freedom of the foreign exchange market it belongs, strictly speaking, to the category of exchange restrictions. Notwithstanding this it is justifiable to class it under a separate heading, not merely because of its great importance but also because, in a way, it constitutes a remedy, or an alternative, to exchange restrictions. There are three kinds of Exchange Clearing:

(1) Unilateral.

(2) Bilateral.

(3) Three-cornered.

The indirect measures of Exchange Control may be classed under four headings:

(1) Import restrictions.
(2) Encouragement of exports.
(3) Barter arrangements.
(4) Embargoes on foreign loans.

(1) Import restrictions may or may not be considered as measures of Exchange Control, according to whether they aim primarily at protecting home trade or whether they aim mainly at safeguarding the exchanges. Very often the Governments have both ends in mind in imposing restrictions on imports. Occasionally, on the other hand, exchange restrictions serve incidentally the purpose of protecting home industries. Import restrictions may take the following forms:

(1) Customs tariffs.
(2) Quotas.
(3) Prohibition of certain imports.

(2) Bounties are given to exports largely in order to stimulate trade. At the same time, as in the case of import restrictions, the authorities have also in mind the support of the exchange. Encouragement of exports may take the following forms:

(1) Subsidies to exports, shipping, etc.
(2) Advantages secured by trade treaties.
(3) Encouragement of exports through differential currencies.

(3) The object of barter arrangements, like that of the encouragement of exports or restriction of imports, may be twofold. In addition to relieving pressure on the exchange through the purchase of indispensable commodities abroad, it may pursue the end of creating a market for home products. Barter may consist of private or official arrangements.

(4) The object of an embargo on foreign loans is often to retain national savings exclusively for inland requirements. At the same time in most cases its primary aim is to safeguard the currency against the effects of lending abroad. The embargo on foreign loans may assume the following forms:

(1) Embargo on public issues.

(2) Embargo on placing securities privately.

(3) Embargo on foreign loans, public or private, unless the proceeds are spent on the purchase of national goods.

(4) Embargo on foreign credits.

In this chapter we do not propose to go into a detailed examination of any of the categories of exchange restrictions. We confine ourselves to giving a definition and classification. The list of headings and sub-headings, formidable as it may appear, cannot claim to be absolutely complete. Day after day new regulations are introduced in some part of the world, and it is quite probable that by the time this book is published several new kinds of Exchange Control may have been adopted. In later parts of the book we shall examine the various methods of Exchange Control in detail. In the meantime the material of this chapter might be helpful to readers of the following four chapters giving a historical account of the application of Exchange Control during and after the war.

CHAPTER III

EXCHANGE CONTROL DURING THE WAR

No apology is required for giving a brief summary of developments in Exchange Control during the war. After all, twenty years have passed since the outbreak of the World War, and a new generation, which has no recollections of the exact nature of the financial developments between 1914 and 1918, has grown up. Even many of those who followed the financial aspects of the war with interest have only hazy recollections of what was actually going on. Looking back upon that period, only the broad outlines of the events are remembered, and details are often forgotten. Owing to the limitations of human memory, some important misconceptions have developed and have gained popularity. One of the most characteristic of them is the notion that the war resulted in an immediate and complete change-over from freedom to control in the sphere of foreign exchanges. In reality the evolution of Exchange Control during the war was not nearly as simple. It came gradually and, in some countries at any rate, it was relatively mild in form, while in no country was it as strict and as complete as the systems adopted in subsequent years.

It is thus incorrect to say that the war resulted in the complete curtailment of the freedom of the exchanges through Government intervention. Nor is it correct to say that before the war exchange movements were entirely free of Government interference. Unquestionably, foreign exchange markets enjoyed a very high degree of freedom. There was, however, in most countries a certain degree of interference with this freedom on the part of the authorities. The gold standard was not absolutely automatic even in Great Britain, and still less in other countries. It was the duty of Central Banks to intervene from time to time in order to safeguard the stability of the currency. We have seen in the previous chapter that they had various normal methods of Exchange Control at their disposal. These methods had come to be considered as a normal part of the monetary system, and had not been regarded as interference with the freedom of exchange movements. To take an example, in countries whose Central Banks pursued a *Devisenpolitik* this was considered part of the normal functions of the Central Banks. In reality it contained the elements of exchange management by intervention, such as was practised by the Exchange Equalisation Fund in Great Britain and by similar official organisations in other countries during the world crisis. The range of fluctuations which the foreign exchange policy of pre-war days aimed at counteracting, was of course very moderate. Economists were none the less aware that foreign exchange policy constituted State intervention, and Knapp, amongst others, welcomed it as such, while the purists of economic freedom mildly criticised it.

Notwithstanding the existence of such a moderate form of intervention in some countries, the working of the gold standard before the war was largely automatic in countries on a gold basis. Most acts of artificial interference with the automatic working of the gold standard resorted to in various countries, aimed at safeguarding the gold reserve in times of pressure

rather than at interfering with exchange movements.
Even in countries which were not on an effective gold
standard there was relatively little interference with
exchanges. The idea of official intervention for preventing a depreciation was almost entirely unknown.
Although there were a large number of international
loans issued during the decades that preceded the war,
their object was not to safeguard the stability of the
exchanges of the borrowing countries. The Governments of Latin America, Russia, the Balkan States,
Japan, China, etc., borrowed abroad, not in order to
support their exchanges but simply because they were
unable to raise in the internal capital market the funds
they required. Incidentally their borrowing contributed
to keeping up their exchanges, but this was by no
means the object of the transactions. Stabilisation loans
and credit arrangements for the support of the exchanges are essentially post-war developments, and
were practically unknown before the war.

Exchange restrictions were also almost entirely unknown in pre-war years. If the normal devices for
maintaining the currency between the gold points
proved to be inadequate in face of strong adverse pressure caused by war or other developments, then the
Governments concerned simply allowed the exchange
to take care of itself. The depreciation of the Latin
American exchanges, for instance, was not accompanied by any deliberate efforts on the part of the
Governments to counteract the tendency by means of
exchange restrictions. Before the war it would not have
occurred to any Government to introduce import duties
or to stimulate exports for the sake of supporting the
exchange. While most of them were keen on safeguarding the home market and expanding in foreign

markets, considerations of exchange rates did not play consciously any part in their policy.

The big creditor countries were not concerned with the possible adverse effect of over-lending upon the exchanges. The conception that any over-lending is bound to produce automatically its natural corrective, was generally accepted. In countries where the authorities reserved the right to interfere with lending abroad, the object of their interference was not to safeguard the exchange but to secure advantages, political or otherwise, in return for authorising the issue of foreign loans.

There was, indeed, no need before the war for any drastic measures of Exchange Control. Both economically and financially the world enjoyed a state of relative equilibrium and, generally speaking, there was nothing to disturb that equilibrium. With the exception of some Latin American countries and, at times, some countries of Southern and Eastern Europe, the exchanges remained stable even in the absence of official interference with the factors affecting them. The world's monetary gold stock was fairly evenly distributed, and free international lending provided subconsciously the correctives to such adverse trade balances as existed. There was no striking discrepancy between the tendencies of price-levels in various countries, and those Governments which had budgetary deficits were mostly in a position to cover them by means of normal borrowing. In such conditions there was no need for any exceptional measures to secure the stability of the exchanges.

The war brought about a fundamental change in this respect. It thoroughly unbalanced the international economic and financial situation. The gold standard was suspended in practically every country. Owing to the abnormal war requirements of the belligerent countries and to the decline in their capacity for the production of ordinary goods, their trade balances showed huge deficits. Owing to the different degrees of inflation in various countries, their price-levels tended to rise in totally different proportions. The equalising influence of free international lending had become curtailed.

In such circumstances the adoption of exceptional measures for the control of the exchanges was an obvious necessity. Notwithstanding this, in no country did the Government produce a cut-and-dried scheme of Exchange Control at the outbreak of hostilities. This was not at all surprising, as the world had no experience of the monetary effects of a modern war. It was at first believed that, so long as the Governments covered their purchases of war material abroad out of exceptional resources, the rest might safely be allowed to take care of itself. In most countries, it is true, there were a number of restrictions imposed on foreign trade, but their object was to safeguard and secure the material required for military purposes. While all belligerent countries prohibited the export of gold from the first day of the war, it was not until much later that Governments began to interfere with exchanges in various ways. Should there be another war it is quite certain that all countries would apply advanced Exchange Control from the beginning. In 1914, however, the necessity for such measures was not realised.

The first measures taken towards the restriction of the freedom of the foreign exchange market were directed in every belligerent country against trading with the enemy. It was not until about 1916 that

general foreign exchange transactions came under restriction. Nor was there any immediate attempt made
at the beginning of the war by any of the Governments to control exchange by means of intervention.
In spite of the absence of control, there was no immediate depreciation of the exchanges of the belligerent countries. In fact, sterling went to a substantial
premium in relation to the dollar, and even the franc
and the mark were quoted at a premium for a while.
The absence of a depreciation of the currencies of
Allies and Central Powers alike in 1914 was due partly
to lack of experience on the part of the public and
partly to the popular belief that the war would be over
in three months. It was not until 1915 that the world
began to realise that the war might drag on for years
and that its expenses were bound to affect the exchanges of the participants. Until then, in spite of their
adverse trade balances, the exchanges of the belligerent
countries were well maintained.

With our to-day's knowledge, we may find it difficult to understand why there was no slump in all
currencies of the belligerent countries in anticipation of
the coming developments which, by jobbing back-
ward, we now regard as having been inevitable. We
must bear in mind, however, that speculators, like the
rest of us, were in 1914 entirely inexperienced as to
the financial consequences of a modern war. The only
modern war on a large scale within living memory was
the Franco-German war of 1870; it left the currency of
the victorious nation unaffected, while the depreciation
of the currency of the vanquished was merely $3\frac{1}{2}$ per
cent. In 1871, during the worst days of the Commune,
sterling was quoted in Paris at 26·10. It is thus not surprising that the world in 1914 did not anticipate any

spectacular slump of the currencies of the belligerent powers.

By 1915 the British authorities were beginning to realise the necessity of placing the exchange under control. This was done in the first place by means of official intervention in the form of pegging the sterling-dollar rate. The New York banking house of J. P. Morgan & Company, acting on behalf of the British Treasury, undertook, during the period between 1916 and 1919, to buy an unlimited amount of sterling at the fixed rate of $4 \cdot 76 \frac{7}{16}$. The funds for this purpose were supplied by the Treasury partly by means of gold shipments and the mobilisation of British dollar securities, and partly by loan operations in the United States. From 1917 onwards it was the United States Government that provided the funds required, by means of inter-allied loans to the British Government. The attitude of the "control" towards the foreign exchange market was entirely passive. J. P. Morgan & Company never intervened actively in the market and never took the initiative in buying sterling. They confined themselves to buying sterling that was offered them for sale, at the fixed price. To use a colloquial expression, dollars were "on tap" at the rate of 4·7640. The tactics adopted by the "control" during the period of 1931–1934 were unknown during the war. There were no attempts at bluffing the market or squeezing bears by means of active intervention. In fact there was no need for such methods, for the stability of the sterling-dollar rate was never doubted, and there was no inducement for bear speculation in sterling. This was because, although the pressure on sterling was considerable, the resources available for its support were generally believed to have been

unlimited. Indeed, never before or since, in the history
of modern finance has any exchange been maintained
so absolutely stable as sterling was against the dollar
during the war. The cost of its stability, apart from
the amounts raised by the British authorities for paying for the supplies purchased abroad was estimated
at some £800 millions.

In addition to control by intervention, the British
authorities also endeavoured to maintain their control
over sterling by restrictions. While the pegging of
sterling in relation to the dollar was absolutely watertight, restrictions were applied in a very mild form.
Their sole object was, in addition to preventing trading
with the enemy—which, strictly speaking, does not
constitute Exchange Control—to prevent an outflow
of British capital. There was no attempt made to check
speculation, for the simple reason that there was no
bear speculation in sterling. Apart from the reason
mentioned above, the absence of speculation was also
due to the absence of the technical facilities which
after the war made it much easier to speculate in
exchanges. The forward exchange market is largely a
post-war creation. Had there been an active forward
exchange market during the war there would undoubtedly have been a good deal more speculative
activity in the neutral countries. As things were, there
was no need for the British Government to worry about
preventing bear speculation in sterling. Nor was there
any attempt made to apply measures of exchange
restriction in order to prevent unwanted imports. To
attain that end indirect methods of Exchange Control
were resorted to. In 1915 the McKenna Duties were
introduced; their object was not to provide protection
to certain British industries but solely to reduce press-

ure on sterling through imports. It is characteristic
of the conception prevailing during the early period of
the war, that rather than interfere with the freedom of
exchanges the Liberal Government then in power preferred to introduce Customs Duties. The same object
could have been achieved, possibly even more effectively, if instead of imposing an import duty of 33 per
cent upon motor-cars, musical instruments, clocks, etc.,
the banks had been instructed not to sell any foreign
exchanges for the import of such goods. This solution
was at that stage apparently unthinkable, and the
British authorities preferred to resort to indirect
methods of Exchange Control. Nor did they impose
any restrictions on the purchase of foreign exchanges
by importers during the more advanced stages of the
war. When submarine warfare made it necessary to
control shipping tonnage, this provided, however, an
indirect method of restricting imports. The authorities
refused to allocate shipping tonnage for any imports
which, from the point of view of the exchange, were
considered undesirable.

The application of exchange restrictions was not too
stringent even within their limited scope of preventing
an outflow of capital. There was, indeed, no necessity
for excessively strict measures because there was no
outflow of capital on a large scale. Apart from considerations of patriotism, lack of experience in invest-
ing abroad otherwise than through the acquisition of
securities issued in London, and the general uncer-
tainty prevailing in every part of the world were in
themselves sufficient effectively to prevent any outflow
of capital on a large scale. Indeed the tendency was
rather in the opposite direction. There was a large
amount of inflow of capital from Allied and even from

neutral countries, seeking refuge in London. In order to discourage such outflow as existed, the banks were required to demand documentary proofs that the foreign currencies purchased by their customers were required for genuine commercial purposes. They were allowed, however, practically a free hand to exercise their discretion. As a rule, the only time the authorities intervened was when they suspected trading with the enemy. According to the experience of foreign exchange departments of banks, the number of cases in which they were inclined to suspect that the purpose of the intended purchase of exchanges was an export of capital was remarkably small. Doubtful cases were referred to the Ministry of Blockade, which was in charge of the exchange restrictions. Exceptional transactions were submitted first to the authorities for approval before the banks were approached.

It is characteristic of the primitive ideas prevailing about Exchange Control in those years, that, for a long time, the authorities did not make any efforts to prevent the export of Bank of England notes. In fact at a time when those notes commanded a premium of 5 per cent and more over the exchange rate, the authorities did nothing to discourage their export to Switzerland. The view was held that the export of bank-notes was beneficial as it had the same effect upon sterling as ordinary exports of commodities. It was only when the notes began to find their way back from the East —where they had been spent by the German army— that steps were taken to stop the traffic.

In France the method of exchange pegging applied was somewhat similar to the one used by Great Britain. The franc was pegged in relation to sterling at a relatively low rate by means of passive as well as active intervention in Paris, operated by the Bank of France. The funds were provided mainly by French borrowing in London and New York, largely in the form of inter-Allied debts. Exchange restrictions were applied in a much stricter form than in Great Britain during the later stages of the war. At the beginning it was considered sufficient to appeal to the patriotism of the banks to discourage any transactions whose object was the transfer of capital abroad. Gradually the French authorities had to adopt official measures of an increasingly strict character. They were, however, much less effective in preventing an outflow of capital, for the simple reason that there was much more inducement for Frenchmen than for Englishmen to send their funds abroad. At one time, in 1918, the British Treasury had to warn the French Treasury that French balances in London had increased considerably and that these balances appeared to be French capital taking refuge in London. It was not, however, until after the war that the outflow of capital from France, in the face of apparently Draconian measures of restriction, began to assume spectacular dimensions.

Among the other Allies, Italy pursued the policy of pegging the lira against sterling. At the end of 1917 the *Istituto Nazionale per i Cambi con l' Estero* was established under the auspices of the Bank of Italy with the purpose of taking charge of the official intervention for maintaining the stability of the lira. In London this Institute operated through twenty-two authorised banks, which bought and sold lire at a fixed price on account of the Institute. Their buying and selling operations approximately offset each other. On the other hand similar methods applied in New York resulted in a huge excess of purchases of lire over sales,

financed out of inter-Allied loans. Like other Allied
countries, Italy did not introduce exchange restrictions
immediately. At a later stage she was experimenting
with the idea of making exchange transactions a monopoly, but subsequently this scheme was abandoned.

In the case of the other Allied powers no noteworthy
attempt was made at pegging. Even though the British,
American, and French Governments granted them
financial assistance on various occasions, these were
used for their official goods purchases abroad. Each one
of them introduced, however, at a more advanced
period of the war, a variety of exchange restrictions.

In Germany no attempt was made to peg the mark
in relation to neutral currencies. From time to time,
when its depreciation began to inconvenience the
authorities, support was provided through the export
of gold. They parted with gold, however, rather spar-
ingly in spite of the accumulation of a large amount
through withdrawals from the internal circulation. The
Reichsbank spent altogether some 450 million marks
on the support of the exchange. This figure is in-
finitely smaller than the huge amounts used up by
Great Britain and her Allies for the same purpose. It
should be remembered, however, that, as the amount
which Germany was in a position to purchase abroad
was restricted, owing to the Allied measures of
blockade, her adverse trade balance was necessarily
smaller than that of the Allies. On the whole it may be
said that no systematic efforts were made to control
the mark by intervention. As a result, the mark fluctuated in neutral countries in accordance with the
prospects of a German victory or of the conclusion of
peace.

It was not until January 1916 that exchange

restrictions were introduced. Even then they assumed a rather mild form until February 1917, when they were considerably reinforced. The fact that even in Germany, the home of State intervention, the Government was reluctant to apply Exchange Control until the more advanced stages of the war duly characterises the strength of the *laissez-faire* conception regarding exchanges inherited from the pre-war period. It was not until after the war that the necessity for efficient Exchange Control was realised.

In the United States exchange restrictions were introduced after 1917, notwithstanding the fact that the trade balance was strongly favourable and that there was no trace of any flight of capital. There was thus no real necessity for any restrictions, but, because the dollar depreciated in terms of several neutral currencies, the American authorities decided to place the foreign exchange market under official control. The control was exercised by the New York representative of the Federal Reserve Board. Intervention in the market confined itself to isolated attempts to bring down the Spanish and other neutral exchanges.

CHAPTER IV

EXCHANGE CONTROL AFTER THE WAR

BETWEEN 1914 and 1918, the civilian population of the belligerent countries, and to some extent even of the neutral countries, had to put up with a great deal of inconvenience, and was longing for the return of the "happy pre-war state of affairs". From an economic point of view, this meant the elimination of every kind of Government interference. Indeed, it was a popular belief that, once hostilities were over, the pre-war freedom of economic life would be completely restored. It was expected, amongst other things, that Exchange Control—whether in the form of intervention or restrictions—would cease soon after the cessation of hostilities. As in so many other respects, the world was disappointed, however, in its expectation of a return to the "happy pre-war days" so far as the freedom of exchanges was concerned. It is true that in some countries—such as the neutral countries, Great Britain, and the United States—Exchange Control was either considerably reduced or altogether eliminated shortly after the war. In the majority of the former belligerent countries, however, it had to be maintained and even reinforced during the years that followed the Armistice.

Indeed, if there was good reason for introducing Exchange Control during the war, there was at least equally good reason for maintaining it in many countries during the period of post-war chaos. Far from settling down to relatively normal conditions,

the world plunged into an orgy of uncontrolled inflation and exchange speculation. Most of the abnormal factors which began to manifest themselves
during the war became accentuated during the first
few post-war years. It was soon realised that the hopes
that the currencies would return to their pre-war
parities after the war would not materialise. On the
contrary, a passing recovery shortly before and immediately after the Armistice was followed by a slump in
all European currencies in terms of dollars. The war
was over, and the world was beginning to pay for it.

It is true that Exchange Control in the form of intervention was materially reduced soon after the termination of hostilities. In March 1919 the pegging of
sterling in relation to the dollar ceased, and simultaneously the pegging of the other Allied currencies
also came to an end. Inter-Allied financial assistance
was discontinued, and each currency was left to fend
for itself. It was not until several years later that a
certain degree of co-operation, in a totally different
form, was restored. Meanwhile, the efforts to bolster
up the various currencies at an uneconomic level had
been abandoned.

Sterling was allowed to take care of itself; although
the exchange restrictions were maintained for a while,
their application was relaxed. Between March 1919
and the return to the gold standard in 1925, the
authorities maintained a strictly neutral attitude in
the foreign exchange market. After the removal of the
exchange restrictions the freedom of the London
foreign exchange market, in the pre-war sense of the
term, was fully restored. Later, however, indirect
Exchange Control was adopted in the form of an
embargo on foreign issues. This embargo was first

adopted in 1924, to facilitate the return of sterling to its old parity. It was removed at the end of 1925 when the authorities believed that the position of sterling was sufficiently consolidated to be left to take care of itself without such indirect control. In the following year, however, owing to the difficulties caused by the general strike and the coal strike, the embargo had to be restored, and was not removed until 1927.

Compared with the embargo introduced during the crisis, it was a very mild and rather inefficient form of indirect Exchange Control. While most issuing houses submitted to the wishes of the authorities and refrained from issuing foreign loans, there was nothing to prevent British companies operating abroad from raising fresh capital by public issues. As for the export of capital in forms other than public issues, it was left entirely free. Issuing houses were at liberty to place large amounts of foreign loans privately, and some of them used and abused this right. The London representatives of American issuing houses placed privately in this country a large portion of their foreign dollar issues. Banks were allowed to grant short-term credits abroad, and in some cases to consolidate existing short-term credits by public issues. As a result of these loopholes the embargo on foreign issues was not a very effective weapon in the armoury of Exchange Control.

In France, the depreciation of the exchange which followed the termination of inter-Allied support induced the authorities to reinforce the existing measures of exchange restrictions considerably. In spite of this, they remained hopelessly ineffective in face of a strong and growing flight from the franc. Nor were the authorities able to check bear speculation in francs, which

D

assumed gigantic proportions between 1923 and 1926. While on paper the restrictions sounded very effective, in practice they were disregarded and evaded by everybody, from Cabinet Ministers and leading bankers to rentiers with a few thousands of francs to spare. It was not until after the stabilisation of the franc in 1926, when many milliards of francs were repatriated, that the extent of the flight of French capital in defiance of the restrictions was realised.

Intervention on a large scale in support of the franc was discontinued early in 1919, the Bank of France preferring to conserve its considerable gold resources rather than attempt to counteract the adverse trend by sacrificing any large part of it. For about five years the French authorities remained neutral in face of the speculative fluctuations of the franc. In March 1924, however, M. Poincaré decided to intervene, and with the aid of credits obtained in London and New York, he succeeded in carrying out one of the most successful bear-squeezing operations in the history of foreign exchanges. Between 1924 and 1926 there was from time to time active intervention, administered with great skill and vigour. In this respect, Exchange Control in France reached a very advanced stage during the period of post-war exchange fluctuations.

In Italy, the National Institute of Exchange continued to follow the fate of the lira with close attention. During the first few troublesome post-war years, no attempt was made to neutralise the effect of political and economic disorder upon the exchange. After the establishment of the Fascist régime, however, the Government began to take an active hand in the foreign exchange market. It introduced stringent exchange restrictions, directed against speculation and the export of capital. The Treasury operated from time to time in the market, while later this task was transferred once more to the Bank of Italy. On repeated occasions, the Institute of Exchange carried out successful bear-squeezing operations, but, owing to the psychological link between the franc and the lira, it was often powerless against adverse movements.

In Germany desperate attempts were made, between 1919 and 1923, to halt the slump in the mark by means of both restrictions and intervention. During the war the extent of intervention was comparatively moderate, though it might have been easy, by drawing upon the Reichsbank's gold reserve more extensively, to limit the depreciation and fluctuations of the mark. After the war, when the mark was evidently doomed, the gold stock was practically depleted in futile attempts to stop the avalanche. From 1921 onwards the exchange restrictions were reinforced to a degree without precedent. Exporters were compelled to surrender the proceeds of their sales abroad, while the purchase of foreign currencies and every kind of payment abroad was subject to Government permit. Indirect Exchange Control was attempted through the limitation of imports, but these efforts were rendered ineffective by the existence of "the hole in the West" —as the possibility of importing through occupied territory was termed.

Notwithstanding the efforts to control the exchange, the flight of capital from Germany went on unabated. This, together with excessive reparation demands on the part of the Allies, and the unfortunate Ruhr adventure of M. Poincaré, resulted in a complete collapse of the mark towards the end of 1923. When Dr. Schacht attempted to stabilise the new currency at one-billionth part of the old mark, his efforts inspired at first no confidence, and at the "black bourse" of Cologne the quotation of the dollar rose from 4·2 billion marks to over 11 billion marks. Thanks to a well-timed intervention, however, the bears were forced to cover in haste, and the operation resulted in a substantial net inflow of foreign currencies to the depleted reserves of the Reichsbank. After the adoption of the Dawes Scheme in 1924, confidence in the reichsmark was sufficiently established to enable the Government to remove the greater part of the exchange restrictions at the end of the year. All the time, however, the reichsmark remained under control, as the Reichsbank operated extensively in the foreign exchange market, and its operations remained a leading factor determining the tendency of the exchanges. The extent of its intervention after stabilisation went far beyond the limits of the normal *Devisenpolitik* in the pre-war sense of the term.

In the Succession States of the Austrian-Hungarian Monarchy, the currency confusion was of a different character from that of most other parts of the world. There the effects of inflation and the flight of capital were complicated by the methods adopted in the various countries for the withdrawal of the old notes of the Austrian-Hungarian Bank. Prior to their withdrawal, these notes were stamped in every country, and a lively traffic soon developed in the notes bearing the various stamps, genuine or faked. The withdrawal of the notes took place in Roumania, Czechoslovakia, Yugoslavia, and Italy at exchange rates particularly favourable to the holders, and there was therefore a strong inducement for importing notes into these countries prior to the withdrawal. A new class of exchange speculators developed, that of the *Valuten-schieber* or "shifter of currencies", who brought the smuggling of notes to a fine art, and against whom the authorities in charge of the Exchange Control in the countries concerned waged a desperate war. Exchange restrictions in these countries assumed mainly the form of preventing the influx of old Austro-Hungarian bank-notes by means of a most rigorous inspection of travellers at the frontiers, which, however, proved futile in face of the ingenuity of the smugglers. Even after the conversion of the notes into national currencies was completed, the exchange restrictions remained in force for a long while.

In some of the countries, notably in Austria, the restrictions resulted in the development of a system which was to assume considerable importance in later years during the economic crisis. It consisted of the differentiation between *Inlandkrone* and *Ausland-krone*, according to whether the amount in question was allowed by the authorities to be transferred abroad. There was a wide discrepancy between the two currencies.

In a number of countries the authorities made desperate attempts to control the exchange rates, not by intervention but by fixing official rates and compelling the buyers and sellers to transact business only on the basis of those rates. This method was already adopted by some of the belligerent countries during the war, and worked then reasonably well, because the depreciation was relatively moderate and because patriotic considerations and the fear of strict measures against the offenders deterred most people from breaking the law. After the war, however, the wider exchange fluctuations increased the temptation to evade the law, and the deterrents no longer operated to the same extent as during the war. As a result, in every country with exchange restrictions a "black bourse" developed. In some cases, its turnover was larger than that of the official market, and the rates quoted certainly reflected the true position more faithfully than official quotations. Notwithstanding strict legislation and its most vigorous enforcement, no Government succeeded in suppressing the "black bourse" completely. Even in Soviet Russia, where the "Ogpu", which was in charge of enforcing the Exchange Control, employed terroristic means for its suppression, and the death penalty was frequently applied, the "black bourse" in Moscow remained in existence. As the Soviet Government monopolised banking, and strict censorship of mail and telegrams made transfers impossible, dealing in bank-notes was practically the only type of foreign exchange operation practised in the unofficial market. In order to make it more difficult, the authorities prohibited the import and export of bank-notes, Russian or foreign. In fact, in 1926 they declared all *chervonetz* notes exported illegally abroad as invalid. Notwithstanding this, the notes found their way back, mainly *via* Persia or the Far East, and were quoted in Berlin, Constantinople, and other markets, at a big discount compared with the official rate. At the same time, foreign currencies commanded huge premiums at the "black bourse" of Moscow.

While during the war Exchange Control worked effectively, it failed to attain its object during the period of post-war currency chaos. The world had in the meantime learnt the science and art of exchange speculation, and the habit of shifting capital from one country to another—a habit which was to play a fateful part in the financial history of later years—had become thoroughly popular. In face of these forces the authorities of most countries proved to be helpless. No sooner did they devise some new method of restriction than their adversaries discovered the loophole through which to circumvent it. The development of a forward exchange market provided speculators with a unique field for their activities. The combined power of speculators all over the world had become a factor of immense importance, and, when the authorities attempted to defeat it, more often than not they got the worst of the encounter.

Nor was exchange control more successful, generally speaking, when it assumed the form of intervention. As in the case of restrictions, lack of adequate experience placed the authorities at a disadvantage in their struggle with market influences. Even in countries such as France, where technically the intervention was managed with remarkable skill, it often failed because of the lack of understanding of the underlying principles that should govern exchange management. It was not until later years that the authorities of all countries were to learn, at the cost of many reverses, that the odds are against them if they try to bolster up the exchange at an abnormal level in face of the fundamental trend of the market.

CHAPTER V

THE PERIOD OF STABILISATION

Post-war financial history may be divided into three periods: that of currency chaos, that of stability, and that of the economic crisis. It is not easy to determine the exact date which separates one period from the other. From a financial point of view, the crisis began undoubtedly in 1931 with the Creditanstalt troubles, which is a distinct enough landmark between the period of stability and that of the relapse into currency chaos. It is much more difficult to find such a landmark between the period of post-war currency chaos and that of post-war stability, for the movement towards currency stabilisation began as early as 1922 and went on until the eve of the crisis of 1931. In fact the Spanish currency did not achieve comparative stability until a number of stable currencies had become unstable once more. It is, nevertheless, safe to regard the stabilisation of sterling as the landmark that separates the period of stability from that of chaos. Admittedly, a number of currencies were stabilised before sterling. In 1922 the Czechoslovakian crown was stabilised; this was followed in 1923 by the stabilisation of the German and Austrian currencies, while in 1924 Hungary achieved stability. When sterling was stabilised several major currencies, the most important of which were the franc and the lira, were still unstable. Notwithstanding this, the date of Great Britain's return to the gold standard constituted a landmark, because

Great Britain set an example which every country endeavoured to follow.

Many people expected that, with the return of stability, Exchange Control would disappear. This assumption was not by any means unreasonable. After all, exchange restrictions, intervention, and the various indirect forms of Exchange Control, were adopted as a result of the lack of stability, so that it was logical to expect that, when stability was restored, there would be no need for them to be maintained. In practice things did not work out in such a simple manner. It was impossible to return to the freedom of the foreign exchange market overnight, and even in the long run it was impossible, generally speaking, to return to freedom in the full pre-war sense of the term. Indeed, the act of stabilisation itself was only achieved in practically every case as a result of the arrangement of exceptional Exchange Control measures.

In the majority of cases exchange restrictions were not lifted immediately after the legal stabilisation of the currency. It was feared that a too sudden return to freedom after many years of restrictions might lead to capital movements which might endanger the newly achieved stability. In most countries the Governments considered it advisable to maintain restrictions, even though in a modified form, for several years after stabilisation was carried out. In every country, however, the Governments set themselves as an ideal the complete removal of exchange restrictions. By 1931 most countries had, in fact, achieved this object.

While the movement towards stabilisation was accompanied by a gradual removal of exchange restrictions, Exchange Control in the form of intervention actually increased, especially during the initial period.

This was only natural, for it was too much to expect the public to trust implicitly in the success of the stabilisation schemes, especially as in several cases— such as that of the zloty and the Belgian franc—the first attempt had failed after a short interval. In order to maintain the stability of currencies pending a return of confidence, it was necessary for the authorities in most countries to draw upon their resources to support the exchange. These resources were provided in practically every case through international loans and credits. Between 1923 and 1929 a series of stabilisation schemes were adopted under the auspices of the League of Nations and with the active co-operation of the leading Central Banks. Although these schemes differed from each other in detail they all included arrangements for the issue of a stabilisation loan and the conclusion of a stabilisation credit. It was with the aid of these resources that the authorities of the countries concerned were placed in a position to intervene in support of their exchanges.

There were several exceptions to this rule. For instance, France succeeded in stabilising the franc without any external assistance. Portugal, with much weaker resources of her own, can boast of a similar achievement. In the case of Great Britain, a big stabilisation credit was arranged in the United States, but it was not actually drawn upon. The stability of sterling was maintained without any intervention until the summer of 1931. Great Britain was also among the few countries which achieved stabilisation without any exchange restrictions either before or after the change. Exchange restrictions in Great Britain were discontinued shortly after the end of the war, and it was not until after the suspension of the gold standard that they were reintroduced for a short while. On the other hand indirect Exchange Control was practised in the form of an embargo on foreign loans. We pointed out in the previous chapter that it was thanks to this embargo that sterling was raised to its old parity in 1925. Although the embargo was far from complete and therefore not very effective, it certainly assisted the authorities in their task of getting over the initial difficulties in 1925, and especially in weathering the adverse trend caused by the strikes of 1926. In spite of the application of the embargo, it may be said that Exchange Control was applied in a very mild form in connection with the stabilisation of sterling.

The same cannot be said concerning the franc. Although France succeeded in stabilising her currency without any external assistance—the credits granted for intervention purposes in 1924 were repaid in the following year—this was because France herself possessed a big reserve in the form of French capital which had taken flight abroad during the troubled years. When in 1926 the firm measures taken by Monsieur Poincaré created optimism regarding the prospects of the franc, there was a wholesale repatriation of these funds. To avoid an unwanted appreciation of the franc beyond the level that was eventually chosen as the definite new rate of stabilisation, the Bank of France bought huge amounts of foreign currencies. It was thanks to its intervention that the franc was maintained at an excessively low level compared with its economic parity. As a result of this intervention the French authorities succeeded in accumulating a large reserve in the form of balances in London and New York. These reserves subsequently played an important part in financial and political history. They enabled the French authorities to intervene in the foreign exchange market as and when they considered it to be in accordance with their interest to do so.

In Germany the authorities retained control after the stabilisation of the reichsmark was achieved. It was not until 1926 that the last restriction was removed. During the period that followed the stabilisation, draconian measures were maintained to prevent free dealings, and even the biggest banks had to pay the penalty if they were caught circumventing the regulations. The Reichsbank continued to operate regularly in the foreign exchange market throughout the period of stability, although it is not easy to say when its operations amounted to actual intervention and when they were merely a matter of routine in pursuance of *Devisenpolitik* in the pre-war sense of the term.

Generally speaking, at no time during the period of post-war stability was freedom of exchanges, in the pre-war sense of the term, restored. Most Central Banks were more active in pursuing a foreign exchange policy than before the war. Those Central Banks which before the war kept aloof from exchange operations had to adapt themselves to the changed situation, while those which already before the war pursued a foreign exchange policy adopted a more active attitude during the period of post-war stability. Generally speaking, the gold standard was much less automatic than in pre-war days, and there was much wider scope left for the management of the exchange.

During the period of stability Exchange Control was practised, directly or indirectly, in many instances through international co-operation. Although co-operation between Central Banks was not altogether a post-war development—from time to time Central Banks assisted each other on exceptional occasions before the war—it was only after the war that the declared object of that co-operation was mutual assistance in maintaining the stability of exchanges. On more than one occasion the bank-rate policy of a country was determined in order to assist another country in maintaining the stability of its exchange. The reduction of the New York bank rate in August 1927 was the best-known example of this type of Exchange Control through international co-operation. There were also instances of direct intervention in support of the exchange of another country. For example, the Federal Reserve Bank of New York adopted the practice of buying sterling bills to support sterling.

The establishment of the Bank for International Settlements was an innovation of importance in the sphere of Exchange Control through international co-operation. It is true that the extent to which it actually collaborated in Exchange Control was relatively small. Its organisation provided, however, unprecedented possibilities for Exchange Control. It was in connection with the Bank for International Settlements that the idea of an international Exchange Clearing was first raised. The board and management of the bank was, however, against what at the time was regarded as a revolutionary innovation. It arrived at the decision that it was not desirable for the bank to aim at reducing the volume of dealings in the open market. On the basis of this conception the suggestion that the bank should become an international Clearing House for exchange operations was rejected. It was only in a much less ambitious form that the bank consented to act as a Clearing House. As a number of Treasuries had accounts with the bank, inter-Allied debt payments and reparations were carried through by transfer from one account to the other. In doing so the bank diverted a certain number of transactions from the foreign exchange market.

The bank also provided the funds, on several occasions, to enable various Central Banks to intervene in support of their exchanges. The investment of the banks' assets involved, of course, a certain amount of foreign exchange business, but this can hardly be said to have had any bearing on Exchange Control. Those who expected that the Bank for International Settlements would become, sooner or later, the controlling factor in the foreign exchange market had to admit, even before the advent of the crisis, that their anticipations had failed to materialise. Even when its resources stood at their highest level they were not nearly sufficient to influence the foreign exchange market materially. In any case it was not only the capacity to influence exchanges that was lacking, but also the will to embark upon any ambitious policy. In spite of the existence of international co-operation between Central Banks, and in spite of the existence of the Bank for International Settlements, Exchange Control remained essentially national in character.

A peculiar form of official interference with exchange rates was adopted in some instances during the period of stability. It consisted of measures the result of which was the shifting of the gold points. Already before the war some Central Banks had resorted to such measures in order to discourage the outflow of gold or to encourage the inflow. During the period of post-war stability the best known of such instances

was that of the refusal of the Bank of England to pay
out fine gold and the simultaneous refusal of the Bank
of France to accept gold of inferior fineness. As a result,
the sterling-franc gold point shifted in favour of France
and sterling depreciated below its normal gold point.
For the technical details of the interesting situation
thus created the author must refer the reader to his
book, *The Fight for Financial Supremacy*, published in
1931. This instance of interference with exchanges
through interfering with the gold points was in itself
of no particular importance as a measure of Exchange
Control, especially as its primary aim was not to affect
the exchanges but to affect gold movements. Its significance from the point of view of Exchange Control
lies in the fact that it constituted a primitive precedent
for the American gold policy adopted at the end of
1933, which was to become one of the most remarkable means of Exchange Control yet seen.

CHAPTER VI

THE period of stability came to an unexpected end in 1931. Following upon the Creditanstalt crisis there was a run on the Central European currencies, in the first place on the Austrian schilling, Hungarian pengo, and the reichsmark. Before long the movement assumed world-wide proportions and each country had to take its turn as the storm centre. In June 1931 a flight from the pound developed, leading to the suspension of the gold standard three months later. Before long the dollar itself was exposed to a run and the Dutch guilder also was subjected to attack. A flight of capital from Japan swept the yen off the gold standard by the end of the year. Although the dollar and the Continental gold currencies resisted the attacks to which they were exposed from time to time in 1932, there was a widespread feeling that sooner or later their turn would come. This presentiment became confirmed, as far as the dollar was concerned, in April 1933. As for the minor currencies such as the Roumanian leu, drachma, dinar, Estonian mark, and the Latin American currencies, withdrawals of credits and adverse changes in trade balances resulted in selling pressure which most Governments found difficult to withstand.

It was to be expected that Exchange Control, which declined during the period of stability, should once more assume greater importance during the crisis. No Government allowed its exchange to depreciate with-

out putting up a fight to save it, in the form of intervention, exchange restrictions, and various other
methods of Exchange Control. In fact, under the
pressure of necessity, the science and art of Exchange
Control has made immense progress since 1931. New
methods have been invented and the old ones improved beyond recognition. There can be hardly any
comparison between the hesitating and primitive
measures applied during the war, and even after the
war, and the elaborate systems applied during the
economic crisis. Whether or not the critics agree with
the principle of Government interference with the
exchanges, they must admit that the system has
certainly been brought to a high degree of efficiency.

The first effect of the currency crisis was increased
intervention. Throughout May, June, and July the
German, Austrian, and Hungarian monetary authorities made desperate efforts to cope with the heavy
buying of foreign currencies caused by the withdrawal
of credits and by the flight of national capital. They
used up a large part of their own resources, and in
addition raised credits abroad to enable them to continue to support their exchanges. In July the British
monetary authorities also decided to intervene in
order to counteract the adverse pressure on sterling.
To that end they contracted external credits to a total
of 130 million pounds. In face of the landslide, however, this amount was exhausted by September 20,
1931, and there was no choice but to abandon intervention and suspend the gold standard. They did not
resume their intervention until February 1932. In the
meantime the object of such purchases of foreign
currencies as they made from time to time, was not
to control the exchange but to accumulate foreign

E

balances for the repayment of their dollar and franc credits.

In February 1932 the British authorities resumed their intervention, this time in order to prevent an excessive appreciation of sterling. To facilitate this task the Government established an Exchange Equalisation Account with initial resources of 175 million pounds. From time to time the authorities intervened throughout 1932 and 1933 in order to prevent either an excessive depreciation or an excessive appreciation. While originally they made many mistakes owing to lack of experience, they gradually developed a technique which earned envious praise abroad and silenced criticism at home.

Exchange Control in Great Britain assumed the form of restrictions as well as that of intervention. These restrictions were adopted after the suspension of the gold standard and were removed six months later. They did not aim at the creation of a watertight system and were not applied with much rigour. Their aim was solely to prevent a flight of British capital abroad. No measures were taken to prevent the withdrawal of foreign capital, bear speculation in sterling, or the purchase of foreign currencies for imports. Even the restrictions on the export of British capital had so many loopholes that they could be easily circumvented by anyone in close touch with the market. In March 1932 the freedom of the foreign exchange market was completely restored, and was jealously safeguarded against any pressure for the adoption of Exchange Clearing or any other restrictive measures.

In addition to intervention and restrictions, indirect methods of Exchange Control were also re-

sorted to. The adoption of a protective customs tariff
pursued the dual aim of protecting home production
and safeguarding sterling against an adverse trade
balance. They may be regarded therefore as measures
of indirect Exchange Control. The embargo on foreign
issues, which operated to some extent already before the crisis, assumed a much stricter form from 1932
onwards. While until then only foreign public issues
were affected by it, in its form adopted in 1932 private
security transactions of considerable magnitude, and
even the issue of new share capital for British companies
operating abroad, were also placed under embargo.

In Germany Exchange Control assumed a totally
different form. After having used up the greater part
of its resources, the Reichsbank was no longer in a
position to intervene effectively in face of the continuous drain. It was therefore decided, in July 1931,
to adopt measures amounting to a partial transfer
moratorium. While the interest on the foreign debt
was allowed to be transferred, capital repayments on
account of the short-term debts were checked. Subsequently the working of the transfer moratorium
was regulated by Standstill Agreements concluded
between German debtors and their foreign creditors.
It was thanks to these measures of Exchange Control
that it was found possible to prevent a collapse of the
reichsmark. At the same time exchange restrictions
were reintroduced in order to check the flight of
German capital. The provisions against the circumvention of these restrictions gradually increased in
severity, and efficiency in their enforcement was also
improved. At the same time various loopholes were
deliberately left in order to encourage the repurchase
of German loans abroad at a low price.

Simultaneously with the adoption of Standstill Agreements and exchange restrictions, a novel system of blocked currencies was established. Foreign creditors, even if they obtained repayment in reichsmarks, were not at liberty to make free use of their balances, which were subject to restrictions that varied according to the origin and nature of the balances. Their holders were only allowed to use their funds for certain definite purposes, such as the purchase and export of certain commodities, or the investment in definite types of securities and real property. The object of these restrictions was to prevent foreign creditors from withdrawing their balances in the form of exports for which Germany would in the ordinary course have obtained payment in foreign currencies. The idea was that these balances should be allowed to be repatriated in a way from which German export trade would derive direct benefit. The result was the development of a complicated system of differential currencies, which was adopted also in a number of other countries, and which will be dealt with in detail in a later chapter.

Exchange Control, which was never completely abandoned in Italy even during the period of stability, was reinforced during the crisis. There was a strong bear attack on the lira in anticipation that it would share the fate of sterling, and to resist it the Italian authorities had to resort to exceptional measures. To some extent Exchange Control assumed the form of increased intervention, though in the case of Italy intervention remained the exception and not the rule. A much more effective weapon of Exchange Control was the establishment of unofficial restrictions. No legislation was passed, but the banks had voluntarily

undertaken to restrict their foreign exchange operations so as to prevent both a flight of capital and bear
speculation in lire. Thanks to the discipline prevailing
in Italy, the unofficial restrictions have been carried
out with the utmost efficiency and have been more
effective than the official restrictions in some other
countries. Indirect Exchange Control was also applied
in Italy in the form of retaliation against any country
which either restricted the import of Italian goods or
retained the proceeds of such imports on blocked
account.

The Japanese authorities made an attempt in 1931
to maintain the gold standard in spite of the pressure
caused by the flight of capital. To that end the Yokohama Specie Bank, which has always been in charge
of the official exchange operations, intervened in the
market to an increased extent, selling the foreign
currencies—mainly dollars—required by the market.
In December these efforts had to be abandoned, and
the yen was allowed to depreciate to a considerable
extent. At the same time exchange restrictions were
applied to prevent the transfer of Japanese capital
abroad.

In the United States, during the various spells of
flight from the dollar between October 1931 and March
1933, the authorities intervened mostly through the
intermediary of the London and Paris branches of the
leading New York banks. They were buying dollars
on a large scale so as to keep the exchange between
gold points and to prevent a provisional depreciation
which might otherwise have taken place owing to the
inadequate facilities for the transport of gold. In normal circumstances such intervention was unnecessary,
for gold movements automatically maintained the

exchanges between gold points. During the crisis, however, the transfer of vast liquid funds from one centre
to another resulted in gold movements with which the
existing transport and insurance facilities were unable
to cope. Hence the necessity of intervention.

After the suspension of the gold standard in the
United States the authorities ceased to intervene and
allowed the dollar to depreciate. In fact they openly
declared themselves in favour of a policy of depreciating the dollar. Somewhat inconsistently, at the same
time, they adopted measures of exchange restriction in
order to prevent the export of capital as well as bear
speculation in dollars abroad. The restrictions were
very far from water-tight and failed to achieve their
object. Until October 1933 the depreciation of the
dollar was largely due to the anticipation of official
measures tending to bring about a depreciation. In
October, however, the authorities began to take an
active hand in deliberately engineering further depreciation. Instead of intervening in the foreign exchange market to achieve that end, they adopted a
new policy of fixing a buying price for gold above its
world-market price. At first this policy was ineffective
as it was not accompanied by free imports of gold, and
the authorities themselves did not purchase a sufficient
amount of gold abroad to make their official buying
price effective. When, however, the buying price was
raised consistently the anticipation of a further rise
resulted in a depreciation of the dollar even beyond the
figure justified by the gold buying price. In November
the authorities stopped raising the gold price, with the
result that the dollar became once more overvalued
compared with its gold parities. All the time there was
thus a considerable discrepancy between these provi-

sional gold parities of the dollar and the actual exchange rate. It was not until February 1934 that the gold price was made to become effective by authorising private arbitrage to ship gold. Within a few weeks a huge amount of gold was shipped from Europe and a new buying price at last became effective.

A large number of countries in Central and South-eastern Europe, as well as in Latin America, introduced exchange restrictions during the crisis. In addition to aiming at the prevention of the outflow of capital and of bear speculation in the national currency, most of these restrictions aimed at the prevention of luxury imports and the payment of foreign debts. While some countries, such as Germany, confined themselves to the prevention of payment of debts contracted prior to the adoption of restrictive measures, other countries went further and blocked even the purchase price of current imports. As a result a complete deadlock in foreign trade was threatening. To overcome it a new method of Exchange Control was devised and adopted by a number of countries under the name of Exchange Clearing. Agreements were concluded between a number of countries by which the exporters of the countries concerned were repaid out of the proceeds obtained from importers of goods from the debtor country, cutting out the foreign exchange market entirely. Thus the importers of country A from country B, instead of transferring the purchase price, had to pay it in to a special account kept by the Central Bank of Country A, and the exporters of country A to country B obtained payment from that account.

Between 1931 and 1934 a large number of such bilateral agreements were concluded. The countries which were particularly keen on it were the Danubian

States, the Balkan States, Switzerland, Germany, and, to a less extent, France, Italy, Belgium, and several Latin American States. A large and increasing proportion of international trade is now carried on under the system of Exchange Clearing. While at first it was regarded as just another form of exchange restriction, in many countries it has gradually come to be regarded as a way to overcome exchange restrictions. Its importance is beginning to be realised all over the world to an increasing degree. We propose to deal with its technical and economic problems, as well as with the prospects of the system, in later chapters. Here let it be sufficient to point out that during a little over two years the system has assumed great importance among the methods of Exchange Control.

Indirect methods of Exchange Control have also been adopted all over the world to an increasing extent. Even the French authorities, who are very anxious to maintain the principles of the pure gold standard and would not think of adopting any kind of direct Exchange Control, have formulated their foreign trade policy with the object of safeguarding the stability of the franc. This is the declared object of the system of quotas with which France is endeavouring to prevent a deterioration of her trade balance. The variety of new customs duties, quotas, prohibitions, import licences, and other restrictions adopted by almost every country, pursues largely the same end.

We have thus seen that the period of the economic crisis has witnessed the development of Exchange Control into a highly complicated system working with a variety of direct and indirect methods. Financial literature has failed, so far, to keep pace with the development sketched in the brief historical survey

given in the last four chapters. In the subsequent
chapters we propose to examine the material provided
by twenty years' history of Exchange Control, to
describe its technical details and to analyse critically
its underlying principles.

CHAPTER VII

THE SCOPE OF EXCHANGE CONTROL

In Chapter II. we defined Exchange Control as an effort on the part of the authorities to interfere with the normal factors affecting exchange rates. Such interference may have for its object to cause a wanted rise or fall in the value of the national currency, or merely to prevent an unwanted rise or fall. The efforts of Monsieur Poincaré in 1924 to raise the value of the franc by squeezing the bears is a characteristic example of Exchange Control aiming at an appreciation of the national currency. The gold policy adopted by the United States towards the end of 1933 is an example of Exchange Control aiming at the depreciation of the currency. The defence of sterling in 1931 is an example of Exchange Control for the prevention of a depreciation in the currency, while the intervention of the Exchange Equalisation Fund in the early months of 1932 and 1933 was an instance of Exchange Control aiming at preventing an unwanted appreciation of the currency.

Among the various types of Exchange Control, intervention can be, and has been, used for each one of the four objects of Exchange Control. It can be used for causing a rise or a fall, and also for preventing a rise or a fall. Exchange restrictions, on the other hand, have only been used for preventing an unwanted fall or causing a desired rise. Although theoretically it is possible to restrict an influx of funds in order to cause a fall or prevent a rise of the exchange, this is not known to have been done so far. Gold policy as a means of Exchange Control can only be used for causing a rise or a fall in the exchanges. If it is merely used for preventing a rise or a fall it comes under the heading of normal measures of Exchange Control, which are not within the scope of this book. Exchange Clearing is essentially a passive method of Exchange Control; by its very nature its aim is to maintain the *status quo* and not to cause a change.

Among the indirect methods of Exchange Control, tariff policy may be applied either to cause a rise in the exchange or to prevent a fall. In theory it is possible to remove tariffs in order to prevent a rise in the exchange or to cause a fall, but in practice this has not been done so far. The same may be said to hold good as regards indirect Exchange Control in the form of stimulating exports. An embargo on the export of capital can be applied to cause a rise or prevent a fall of the exchange. With an embargo on the import of capital the opposite effect can be obtained, and this method has been applied for the purpose of preventing a rise or causing a fall of the exchange.

Exchange Control is positive when it aims at preventing a fall or causing a rise. It is negative when it aims at preventing a rise or causing a fall. As in every sphere of human activity, it is much easier to destroy values than to create them. The task of causing a fall or preventing a rise of the exchange is much easier than that of causing a rise or preventing a fall. In order to prevent an exchange from appreciating or to make it depreciate, all that is wanted is to be able and willing to sell an adequate amount of the national currency. In order to prevent a fall in the national currency, or to cause a rise, the use of reserve resources (gold and foreign exchanges) is necessary. While every country has an unlimited source of national currency, its resources of gold and foreign currencies, however large, are limited. The only limits to the extent to which a Government can sell national currency in order to prevent its appreciation or to cause its depreciation, are those which are self-imposed. If any existing restrictions on the expansion of the national currency, legal or otherwise, are removed, the sky is the limit to the extent to which the authorities can operate against a rise or in favour of a fall. They can utilise the resources of the national currency to that end either through intervention or through gold policy.

When it comes to positive Exchange Control the task becomes much more difficult. There is, it is true, a great variety of means at the disposal of the authorities for preventing an unwanted fall or for causing a desired rise. Notwithstanding this, their power against a persistent and strong adverse trend is limited.

From the point of view of the methods by which Exchange Control is operated, we can distinguish three main forms. The mildest form of Exchange Control is when it is operated by means of unofficial advice and moral pressure upon the banks and the market. There is an immense variety of possible degrees of moral pressure, beginning with an appeal to patriotism and ending with threats and reprisals which, in practice, amount to legal restrictions. The "Buy British" movement is an example of the mildest form of moral pressure, while the "unofficial" embargo on foreign loans is an example of its strictest form. The second degree of Exchange Control consists of legal measures without actually establishing a monopoly in exchange dealings. In this case the banks, or a certain number of them, are allowed to deal between each other and with their customers provided that they observe the law. Intervention may also be classed in this category of Exchange Control as it presupposes a certain freedom of the market. The third and most extreme degree of Exchange Control is the establishment of monopoly in exchange dealings. In this case banks, if allowed to operate at all, can only act as intermediaries between their customers and the authorities, and the only legitimate counterpart of any normal supply and demand is the Central Bank or the equivalent authority. In this case the freedom in foreign exchange transactions is completely suppressed. The extreme forms of exchange restrictions and Exchange Clearing may be classed under this heading.

Let us now survey the factors and forces against which Exchange Control is applied. These can be classified under the following headings:

(1) The transfer of liquid balances.

(2) The flight of national capital.

(3) Speculation.

(4) Fluctuation of the trade balance.

(5) Exchange Control by other countries.

The transfer of liquid balances from one centre to another has been one of the principal disturbing influences during the world economic crisis. It has taken the form of capital movements of abnormal magnitude which cannot be expected to be offset by the automatic working of the currency system. It has to be dealt with by special measures of control, either in the form of restrictions—such as the German transfer moratorium in 1931—or in the form of intervention. The movements of these balances may prove embarrassing not only when they leave a country but also when they enter a country. While Exchange Control in the form of restrictions has been applied against the departure of liquid balances, there have been no instances, so far, of the application of exchange restrictions against their influx. The authorities have, however, a very effective weapon to deal with an unwanted influx, in the form of intervention.

The flight of national capital has much similarity to the movements of liquid international balances. In a way it is more dangerous, because the amount of national capital available for export is usually larger than the amount of foreign balances. Exchange restrictions usually deal with national capital more severely than with foreign balances, and owing to the physical presence of its owners the penalties for evasion of the restrictions are more easily enforced. Like the transfer of balances, the flight of national capital can operate in both directions. There can be a flight to the national currency as well as a flight from the national currency.

Speculation is a factor which provides a very wide scope for Exchange Control, both in the form of intervention and in that of restrictions. Provided that a speculative movement is not supported by any wholesale transfer of foreign balances or flight of national capital, the authorities are usually in a position to deal with it without having to use too much of their resources. Efficient methods of exchange restriction in themselves go a long way towards dealing with speculation. If intervention is applied with skilful tactics the success achieved may be out of proportion to the moderate amount required. Unfortunately for the Control, speculation is usually accompanied by some other factor which makes it more difficult to deal with.

Fundamental changes in the tendency of foreign trade are another factor the authorities are called upon to cope with. In normal conditions changes in the trade balance are seldom too sudden, and usually normal methods are adequate to deal with them. If it comes to the worst, there is always a possibility of offsetting an adverse balance by borrowing abroad. In conditions such as have prevailed since 1931, however, disturbances of the trade balance cannot be dealt with with normal weapons, and have to be dealt with by means of Exchange Control. Intervention is hardly a satisfactory way of dealing with a persistently and heavily adverse trade balance. Exchange restrictions are a more adequate means for that purpose. They may assume the form of the rationing of currency to importers according to the supply available, or the blocking of payments for part of the goods imported, or the establishment of Exchange Clearing, or indirect methods of control in the form of tariffs, quotas, export bounties, or barter arrangements.

Exchange Control is applied sometimes in order to counteract the effect of Exchange Control measures employed by some other Government or Governments. If intervention is applied in order to neutralise the effect of intervention by a foreign Government, we are at once confronted with a currency war. Fortunately there has not been, so far, any known instance of such an occurrence. On the other hand it happens frequently that exchange restrictions are applied in response to similar measures introduced in other countries. The principle of reciprocity and the practice of retaliation have a wide scope in the sphere of exchange restrictions. Apart from Great Britain there is, indeed, hardly any country which is prepared to see its citizens victimised by exchange restrictions without retaliating. Very frequently the result of a clash between two countries in the sphere of exchange restrictions is either an Exchange Clearing agreement or a barter arrangement. Indirect methods of Exchange Control in the form of import restrictions or a bounty on exports also very often elicit retaliation.

A question of the utmost importance is what the object of Exchange Control should be. In this respect most experts belong to one of four schools of thought, according to whether they maintain that Exchange Control should be employed for one of the following four ends:

(1) To counteract day-to-day fluctuations.

(2) To counteract speculative influences.

(3) To counteract seasonal and other temporary, though sometimes prolonged, normal tendencies.

(4) To counteract fundamental trends, whether normal or abnormal.

If a currency is not on a gold basis and it is not stabilised in relation to a gold currency, its day-to-day fluctuations may at times be wide enough to become a source of unnecessary embarrassment to trade and finance. Large individual transactions, or the coincidence of a large number of transactions of the same nature, are apt to cause a temporary movement which will upset the calculations of exporters and others. Such movements can as a rule easily be dealt with by intervention. Exchange restrictions may also be helpful by regulating the legitimate cause of such day-to-day movements and by enabling the authorities to know exactly what is going on in the market. In countries where exchange transactions have to be declared, any sudden temporary increase of buying or selling can be met instantaneously. Self-imposed exchange restrictions are sometimes applied for that purpose. For instance, during a period when the British authorities intervened frequently in the market, most London banks notified them in advance if they had some unusually large transaction.

To counteract speculative tendencies is a more difficult task, but, as we said above, so long as speculation is not accompanied by any fundamental tendency the authorities would be in a position to cope with it. If speculation merely consisted of the creation of bear and bull positions, exchange restrictions in themselves would go a long way towards checking it. By forbidding the granting of credits to foreigners in the national currency, short selling can be rendered extremely difficult, expensive, and risky. The same effect can be achieved by compelling the national banks to refuse to buy the national currency in forward dealing. This was done in the case of the Dutch guilder on various occasions. It is more effective, however, to apply intervention simultaneously with exchange restrictions.

To counteract speculative fluctuations is necessary and useful, and nobody except the extreme adherents of *laissez-faire* would object to Exchange Control to that end. On the other hand, the idea of counteracting seasonal influences and other genuine temporary factors meets with more opposition. Many people maintain that, while speculation is an abnormal factor and should be fought with abnormal weapons, normal factors such as seasonal influences should be allowed to take their course. The difficulty is that there is no way of separating seasonal and speculative influences. The anticipation of a seasonal movement results in speculative operations which often accelerate and exaggerate

F

the normal effect of those influences. In themselves, exchange restrictions are not particularly helpful in the attempt to control such fluctuations, unless they are applied in a very strict form. Intervention, in order to be effective, requires much larger funds than it does when confined to counteracting day-to-day fluctuations or speculative tendencies.

While the question whether seasonal tendencies should be interfered with by Exchange Control is open to argument, the weight of opinion is usually against intervention to counteract fundamental trends. Experience has shown, however, that in certain circumstances the authorities were successful in combating even fundamental influences with the aid of Exchange Control. It was unquestionably exchange restrictions in the form of a partial transfer moratorium that saved the stability of the reichsmark in 1931. It was Exchange Control in the form of gold policy that enabled the American authorities to depreciate the dollar to the desired level. In any case, it is always difficult to draw a line between seasonal movements and fundamental trends, and between speculative movements and fundamental trends. In fact, even day-to-day movements might prove to be the forerunners of tendencies of a fundamental nature.

In the following chapters we shall try to examine how far the various types of Exchange Control are suitable to achieve the various tasks assigned to them. The object of a critical examination is twofold. We have to examine the economic aspects of Exchange Control in its various applications, and we have to ascertain whether its technical methods are the right ones for achieving its task.

CHAPTER VIII

THE ECONOMICS OF INTERVENTION

WE pointed out before that in the sphere of Exchange Control practice has advanced far ahead of theory. The various methods of Exchange Control have been initiated, not as the outcome of scientific investigations, but as a result of what was regarded as practical necessity. In the majority of cases the initiation of Exchange Control did not take place at the suggestion of economists; in fact it usually met with opposition on their part. Owing to the essentially practical circumstances of its origin, the initiators of Exchange Control were concerned solely with its immediate causes and consequences. Experience has shown, however, that Exchange Control may become a factor of predominant importance in spheres far beyond its immediate concern. In searching for its deeper-lying causes and far-reaching effects we are bound to realise that, far from being a mere matter of foreign exchange technique, it has become a potent factor in our economic system. For this reason Exchange Control deserves a place of importance in economic science.

Amongst the various methods of Exchange Control the economic aspects of intervention deserve particular attention. While other types of Exchange Control are largely negative, as they consist of restrictions imposed upon the freedom of the market, intervention is essentially a positive action. It implies grave responsibilities on the part of the authorities in charge of intervention, and the extent and nature of these responsibilities are not always adequately realised. The authorities in charge of intervention have to combine the qualities of the foreign exchange dealer thoroughly acquainted with the technique of the market, with those of the economist realising the deeper implications of the action taken.

The frequently recurring necessity for intervention since the war is one of the many signs which indicate that the days of *laissez-faire* are over. The economic religion built upon the dogma that "everything operates in the best interests of mankind so long as the authorities abstain from interfering with economic tendencies" no longer corresponds to requirements, whether it is applied to foreign exchange policy or other spheres of economic policy. Experience has proved over and over again that in our changed conditions adverse tendencies, far from carrying their own corrective, as the advocates of *laissez-faire* state, frequently inaugurate vicious circles which can only be broken by artificial interference. These adverse tendencies assume nowadays unprecedented dimensions, and the policy of allowing them to take their course until they can produce their natural correctives can no longer be applied without causing immense losses and sufferings during the "transition period".

As an example of the failure of *laissez-faire* to produce satisfactory results in present-day circumstances, we may remember that it has been a classical rule that an adverse trade balance automatically corrects itself if allowed to bring about a depreciation of the exchange. Under existing conditions, however, owing to import restrictions applied by most countries, and also to the greater degree of elasticity of the economic system of

several commercial rivals of Great Britain, sterling
would have had to be allowed to depreciate to a very
great extent before the desired equilibrium could be
established—if, indeed, it could be established at all
by such means. An excessive depreciation of sterling
would have accentuated deflation, and would have
aggravated the world crisis. It was, therefore, wise to
throw the classical rule overboard by seeking to restore
the trade balance through import duties, and at the
same time to attempt to check the downward trend
of sterling at the end of 1932 and of 1933 by the
application of intervention, in defiance of the principles
of *laissez-faire*.

It was equally wise to try to prevent an appreciation
of sterling when market influences tended to raise the
rate too high early in 1932 and 1933. Admittedly, an
exaggerated appreciation of sterling would set into
motion the corrective influences which, in accordance
with the classical rules, would tend to restore the rate
to a more normal level. As, however, these "corrective
influences" would have meant a falling off of our
exports, and an increase in unemployment, all but the
most fanatical adherents of *laissez-faire* readily forgive
our authorities for having employed intervention as an
alternative solution.

There are still a few die-hard orthodox economists
who maintain that, instead of applying intervention,
the abnormal tendencies of the exchange should be
counteracted by the normal devices of Central Bank
policy—that is, by changing the bank rate and by contracting or expanding the volume of currency, and
credit. As tendencies in the exchange in both directions
are remarkably strong, this would mean unusually
violent fluctuations in interest rates and monetary

resources, which would hardly contribute towards a recovery of trade. If, for no matter what reason, sterling developed a weak tendency, the deflationary measures suggested by orthodox economists might not even be sufficient to prevent a depreciation; but even if they are sufficient, the sacrifice involved would hardly be worth the result, which could well be attained with the aid of intervention.

Capital items, such as the transfer of foreign balances or the flight of repatriation of national capital, have assumed an unprecedented importance in the foreign exchange market. It would be a mistaken policy to apply against them methods which were devised mainly to deal with current items. It has been suggested sometimes that, by applying deflationary measures during the summer of 1931, our authorities might have saved the pound, as by forcing prices down they could have improved our trade balance sufficiently to counteract the adverse trend. Considering that within three months something like £200 millions were withdrawn on capital account, it is difficult to imagine how the pressure could have been counteracted by influencing the items of the current trade balance; as a great part of our imports is inelastic, our exports would have had to be trebled or quadrupled at a moment's notice, which is simply unthinkable to anyone with any practical sense. Obviously, capital items such as the outflow of foreign funds on a large scale can only be dealt with by extraordinary measures of official intervention. The reason why intervention failed to save the pound in 1931 was that the resources at the disposal of the authorities were inadequate to cope with the wholesale capital withdrawals taking place ; had they possessed sufficient resources they could have main-

tained the gold standard. On the other hand, the
application of the orthodox devices would have been
incapable of saving the pound even if they had been
applied to an extreme degree.

Another reason why intervention has become a
necessary part of Central Banking policy is that the
working of normal corrective influences is greatly
handicapped. As a large part of our short-term credits
and long-term investments abroad is frozen, it is impossible to call them back in support of sterling by an
increase of the bank rate. This may be a temporary
state of affairs, but is likely to recur on the occasion of
the next crisis.

Usually the declared object of intervention is to
counteract speculative influences. In the narrower
sense of the term, speculative activity in an exchange
means the creation of long or short positions. The
primary task of the authorities in charge of intervention is to prevent these activities from affecting the
exchange. The application of certain technical devices
enables the authorities to render speculation of such
kind extremely difficult and risky, if not altogether
impossible. In many quarters, however, the view is
held that it should not be the aim of the authorities to
kill speculative activity altogether by means of intervention, for it is pointed out that speculators sometimes fulfil a very useful task in the foreign exchange
market. Without them there could be no active forward exchange market, and even the market in spot
exchanges would be highly unsatisfactory but for the
compensating influence of speculation. Thus, if at a
given moment the volume of non-speculative supply
of a currency in the international market is in excess
of the non-speculative demand, it is the rôle of the

speculators to take up the excess supply—at a price, of course, which offers attractive prospects for appreciation. If speculation is rendered extremely difficult and risky, the same surplus of supply over demand tends to bring about a much stronger depreciation. This is illustrated by the example of Italy; speculation in the lira is, thanks to the intervention of the authorities, almost impossible. Thus, when in November 1932 there was a surplus supply of lire offered in the market as a result of certain exceptional transfers, and the authorities decided to allow it to produce its effect, it brought about a depreciation of the lira entirely out of proportion to the relatively modest amount involved. Notwithstanding this consideration, the advantages of keeping speculation well under control more than outweigh its disadvantages.

The term speculation in a broader sense includes not only the creation of long or short positions, but also the actual international transfer of funds for the purpose of benefiting by, or escaping the consequences of, an anticipated exchange movement. It is against speculation in this broader sense that intervention is usually directed; for it would be not merely futile, but decidedly disadvantageous, even if it were possible, to eliminate bears and bulls while abstaining from counteracting the effects of an inflow or outflow of foreign funds. After all, such capital movements usually widen the discrepancy between actual supply and demand in the market, and it is either the authorities or speculators who have to absorb the surplus or make good the deficiency. Intervention has to be applied indiscriminately against tendencies brought about both by speculation in the narrower sense and by the movement of funds.

The existence of huge floating funds, wandering restlessly from centre to centre, has charged Central Banks with a new responsibility: that of neutralising the effect of these movements upon the national currency. To that end, it is the duty of Central Banks to take up the exchange sold on the occasion of the inflow of such funds, so as to have it in readiness to resell whenever the funds choose to leave the country. Unless this is done, the inflow will result in an unwanted appreciation of the exchange. What is more, as a result of its overvaluation, the national currency will become highly vulnerable, and any adverse factor will produce an exaggerated effect. Having failed to accumulate foreign currencies, the Central Bank is faced with a choice between satisfying the demand for foreign exchange out of its own reserve or allowing the national exchange to depreciate under the pressure of the withdrawal of funds. The disadvantages of this course are only too obvious. Even if a country is on the gold standard and the movements of floating funds cannot materially affect the exchange, the influx and efflux of gold thereby caused unsettles the money market and constitutes a general disturbing influence. In countries which are not on a gold standard it causes wide exchange movements, precisely of the kind which intervention could and should prevent.

Before the crisis London held permanently foreign balances running into hundreds of millions of pounds. Their owners and their composition may have changed constantly, but the limits within which their total amount fluctuated must have been relatively moderate. Thus, it was justifiable to regard a high percentage of these funds as part of the permanent resources of London; there was no need for making provision for the withdrawal of more than a relatively small percentage. The crisis has, however, changed the situation in this respect. Since July 1931 every pound sent here on overseas account represents a potential withdrawal, and should be treated accordingly. As the counterpart of these funds represented by the short-term credits we granted to foreign borrowers has either been repaid or has become frozen, the only way to provide for the contingency of withdrawals is to cover these balances adequately through the acquisition of equivalent foreign balances by the Central Bank. To that end, whenever there is an additional inflow of foreign funds the official foreign exchange reserve has to be increased accordingly. As the Bank of England obtains from all banks the figures necessary to estimate the amount of foreign balances in London, it is in a position to judge the magnitude of its reserve requirements, which should no longer be determined by the amount of the note issue, but by the potential withdrawals on foreign account.

To acquire the equivalent of the inflow of foreign funds is not a luxury, but a necessity. If the Bank of England's foreign exchange reserve increases by, say, £20 millions, while the amount of foreign balances in London increases by twice that amount, its position has not become stronger, but weaker as compared with what it was before the increase. This fact is not generally realised. In April 1932, when the flight to the pound resulted in a considerable increase in the official foreign exchange reserve, it was regarded as a permanent increase in our resources. Hence the absurd suggestion made at the time in some quarters, to remove the recently imposed import duties because "now that foreign funds are flowing in we can afford to import in excess of our exports". There may be hundreds of arguments for and against the removal of import duties, but to suggest that they should be removed so as to consume the proceeds of the short-term credits granted to us by foreigners subject to withdrawal at a moment's notice is too fantastic to be taken seriously. It duly illustrates the ignorance that prevails as to the way in which floating foreign balances have to be treated. It is one of the foremost objects of exchange intervention to enable the authorities to acquire the approximate equivalent of the foreign funds which enter this country.

Although the declared object of intervention is merely to counteract the effect of day-to-day movements and speculation—in its broader sense—upon the exchange, the authorities may often feel tempted to make use of it in pursuance of their general monetary policy. In theory the ideal solution would be to eliminate speculative influences and to allow genuine economic tendencies to take their course in determining the level of the exchange. Unfortunately, it is impossible to determine how far a buying or selling pressure on the exchange is due to genuine economic causes and how far merely to speculation. Thus, the authorities have to take a view as to the level which corresponds to the economic parity of the exchange, and have to use the weapon of intervention to maintain it at that level. In doing so, they are liable to error, and may bolster up the exchange artificially at an untenable level. Such errors are inevitable; what matters is that they should not be committed deliberately. If the authorities feel they are in a strong position they may feel tempted to use the weapon of intervention for raising the exchange, for considerations of prestige, to an unduly high level, in the hope that the economic parity will subsequently adjust itself to this new level. This would amount to the repetition of the mistake committed by Great Britain in 1925, which should be avoided. Taking a long view, it is equally unadvisable to use intervention for maintaining the currency at an unduly low level. Such a policy might accentuate international deflation, or it might lead to an international depreciation race; in either case it would prolong and aggravate the crisis.

Regarded purely from the point of view of foreign exchange policy, intervention is beyond doubt amply justified. Provided that the resources available for its purposes are adequate and provided it is managed skilfully, it is undoubtedly an effective weapon of Exchange Control. Moreover, the interference with the foreign exchange market caused by intervention is much less unpopular than in the case of almost any other form of Exchange Control. For this reason opposition to the idea of the application of this method of Exchange Control is negligible and easily overcome. Indeed, it may be said that intervention has come to be regarded as a recognised part of our monetary system.

We may now go a step further and examine whether intervention is justified from the point of view of its general effects. Although its immediate object is to affect the exchange rates, it is liable to produce, directly or indirectly, far-reaching effects on various spheres of our economic system. In examining its effects it is necessary to discriminate between the effect of the stability or movement of the exchange rates caused by intervention, and the effect of the operations by which stability or movement of exchanges are caused.

The effects produced by an exchange rate that is brought about or maintained by intervention depends largely upon the nature of the tendencies against which intervention is utilised. If the authorities intervene merely in order to counteract speculative or seasonal fluctuations, the effect of maintaining a stable exchange rate is more or less the same as the maintenance of stability by no matter what other means. If the level at which the exchange rate is maintained, thanks to intervention, corresponds to its economic parity, then intervention merely fulfils the functions fulfilled before the war by the normal working of the gold standard. If, however, as a result of intervention the exchange is removed from its economic parity, the action produces totally different effects.

The pegging of the sterling-dollar rate during the war provides a characteristic example of the abnormal effects produced by intervention aiming at bolstering up an exchange above its economic parities. Between 1915 and 1918 the exceptional conditions created by the war in Great Britain tended to raise internal prices. If sterling had been allowed to take care of itself, or if intervention had confined itself to counteracting speculative excesses, the sterling-dollar rate would have moved to a figure roughly representing its economic parity. As it was, sterling was artificially maintained by intervention above its economic parity. As prices in Great Britain were rising and the sterling-dollar rate was pegged, as a matter of simple arithmetics it was inevitable that prices in the United States should also rise, although the conditions which caused prices to rise in Great Britain did not exist in the United States. A rise in prices in the United States was then un-desirable both from an American and a European point of view. The example illustrates therefore that, even though intervention may be successful from the point of view of foreign exchange policy, it can be harmful from a general point of view if its aim is to counteract fundamental tendencies.

In the majority of cases attempts at counteracting fundamental tendencies by intervention were not successful. In Germany after the war the occasional intervention of the Reichsbank to check the depreciation of the mark failed to achieve its end, even from the point of view of foreign exchange policy, and was unable to check the rise in prices. Had Germany possessed a huge gold and foreign exchange reserve she might have been able to bolster up the mark for some years, in which case internal inflation, coupled with the stability of the mark, would have caused world prices to rise. In France between 1926 and 1928 the franc was maintained by intervention at an undervalued level. As the exchange was not allowed to express the ratio between French prices and world prices, and prices in France were not allowed to adjust themselves to world prices, the result was a fall in world prices to adjust themselves to French prices—a most undesirable development which was largely responsible for the crisis.

The British foreign exchange policy during 1932 and 1933 aimed at preventing, by intervention, unduly wide fluctuations of the exchange. The result of this policy was favourable to British prices which were maintained comparatively stable. It was unfavourable, however, for world prices which were caused to fall as a result of the undervaluation of sterling. Had the level at which sterling was maintained through intervention been in accordance with economic parities the adverse effect upon world prices would have been avoided. Unfortunately, lack of adequate resources prevented the British authorities from maintaining sterling at its economic parity.

The effect on production of the exchange rate at which a currency is maintained by intervention largely depends upon its effect on prices and on foreign trade. Undervaluation tends to stimulate production and trade while overvaluation acts as a handicap. The advantages of intervention are essentially temporary, not merely because in the long run prices and exchanges tend to become adjusted to each other, but also because other countries are likely to follow the example so that the undervalued currency of to-day might become an overvalued currency to-morrow. Taking a long view, the economic effect of maintaining a currency at a wrong level by intervention can only be disadvantageous to everybody concerned.

Hitherto we have been dealing with the effects of the choice of the exchange rate by the authorities in charge of intervention. Let us now examine the effects of the operations necessitated by intervention. The purchase and sale of foreign currencies and gold on a large scale is bound to affect both the internal and the international situation. Generally speaking it may be said that the purchase of gold and foreign exchanges on a large scale in connection with intervention tends to produce inflationary effects at home, while the sale of gold and foreign currencies by intervention tends to result in deflationary effects. Much depends, of course, upon the method of financing the intervention. Much depends also upon the degree to which the economic system of the country concerned is receptive towards an expansion of currency and credit. During a period of economic depression, when the supply of credit exceeds the demand, the result of such expansion is merely a plethora of short-term funds and a decline of interest rates. The inflationary effects of intervention would not then make themselves felt too plainly upon the price-level and production. The same is true of the deflationary effect of the sale of gold and foreign currencies by the authorities. In times when the credit resources of the country are more or less fully employed, such operations would produce a deflationary effect. If, however, there are ample idle funds the contraction caused by intervention will produce no material effect upon prices.

As for the international effects of the operations connected with intervention, it is necessary to discriminate between transactions in gold and in foreign currencies. So long as intervention is confined to the purchase of foreign currencies it tends to bring about international inflation, for, while the financing of intervention tends to cause inflation at home the acquisition of large balances abroad tends to cause inflation in the foreign countries concerned. Intervention thus tends to result in the duplication of credit resources in the same way as the operation of gold exchange standard did during the period of post-war stability. Should, on the other hand, the authorities in charge of intervention convert the foreign balances purchased into gold, by withdrawals from the Central Banks of the countries concerned, the international effect of the operation would tend to be decidedly deflationary. In theory the loss of gold by one country means the gain of gold by the other, and the contraction of credit in the one country should be offset by the expansion of credit in the other. In practice, however, the contraction caused by the efflux of gold is usually larger than the expansion caused by the influx.

From a political point of view the effects of intervention are also of importance. While the intervention policy of a relatively small country affects the international situation to a relatively small extent, that of one of the leading countries tends to produce international effects the importance of which cannot be over-emphasised. At present there are three countries which are of predominant importance in the sphere of international finance: Great Britain, France, and the United States. We have seen that the foreign exchange policy pursued by France after 1926 resulted in the accumulation of huge balances which played an immensely important part during the following years. In 1932 and 1933 the position of London was somewhat similar to that of Paris in 1926. The fact that we are not on the gold standard, and that there are a large number of countries which have linked the fate of their currencies to that of sterling, increases the international importance of our foreign exchange policy and its chief weapon—intervention. London still possesses a remarkable magnetic force which attracts foreign capital as soon as the outlook for sterling slightly improves, or as soon as the prospects for some other currency become less favourable. By pegging sterling at a low level our authorities are in a position to accumulate huge reserves. The result of this position is the acquisition of immense power in the international money market. If used for selfish political ends, as was the case with France between 1929 and 1932, this power may become a dangerous and destructive influence. If, however, it is used in a constructive spirit, it may be highly beneficial to all concerned.

G

The political significance of intervention has declined considerably since the practice of acquiring and holding foreign balances in connection with intervention has been abandoned. Now that it has become a rule to convert immediately into gold any foreign balances acquired through intervention, the authorities of the intervening country are no longer in the same position as they were before to help other countries and to use their assistance as a bargaining weapon. At the time when they were prepared to hold foreign balances they were in a position to grant invaluable support to any foreign currency which was in difficulties. During 1932 and 1933 the effects of a flight from the dollar and from the franc were largely counteracted by the operations of the Exchange Equalisation Fund. Unfortunately the British Government never sought to use this assistance as a bargaining counter, and it was given freely and without any counterpart. The possibility of obtaining valuable concessions in return for it existed, however, even though it was not made use of. At present, however, it no longer exists, because to support a currency with the aid of gold withdrawn from that country is no service to the country concerned.

Intervention, nevertheless, still constitutes political power inasmuch as it enables the Government concerned to bargain about the exchange rate. By agreeing to prevent depreciation beyond a certain point a Government might obtain most valuable concessions in a trade agreement. Since the suspension of the gold standard by the United States, and more particularly since the creation of an American equivalent to the British Exchange Equalisation Fund, this advantage ceased to be a British monopoly. Should France and other countries follow the British example, the bargaining value of intervention will depend upon the strength of the respective resources and the skill with which they are handled.

CHAPTER IX

THE TECHNIQUE OF INTERVENTION

THE position of a Government or a Central Bank as active operator in the foreign exchange market differs very greatly, and in many respects, from that of any other dealer. The amount of its operations is, as a rule, larger than that of even the largest private dealers. In many ways it is at an advantage against other operators. It possesses larger resources than any individual operator or group of operators. Although its resources may at times be outweighed by those of all operators combined, in practice the number of dealers who consciously join forces in the foreign exchange market at any given moment is always relatively small. The authorities, thanks to the unity of their command over their resources, are thus at an advantage against a divided market. Moreover, they are often in possession of inside information about factors affecting the value of currency, which information is not, as a rule, available for outsiders. Above all, they know, or ought to know, what their policy is, while the market is necessarily groping in the dark—especially in countries where leakage of information is the exception and not the rule. From this point of view, the American authorities could hardly be said to be always at an advantage *vis-à-vis* the market.

On the other hand, in many ways the authorities in charge of intervention are at a grave disadvantage. They usually work with committees to decide upon

84

the policy and tactics to be adopted, and it takes some time for them to make up their mind during critical periods when every moment is precious. This disadvantage can be overcome if the operation of intervention is placed in the hands of a single person with wide powers of decision, within the limits of the general policy laid down by the Government. Another point in respect of which the authorities are at a disadvantage, especially at the beginning of their activities, is lack of adequate experience. They have to learn their lessons and have to pay the price for them.

Official intervention in the foreign exchange market may be either passive or active. Passive intervention usually aims at maintaining the exchange at a given rate, at which the bank or banks in charge of the operations are prepared to buy or sell foreign currencies. According to this method, the authorities and their agents do not go out of their way to operate in the market. They do not take the initiative in buying or selling foreign currencies, but are prepared to buy or sell them at a given rate if anyone offers them or wants them, and if nobody else is prepared to operate at a more favourable rate. To use the colloquial expression popular in the foreign exchange market, the currency or currencies in question are "on tap".

Active intervention, on the other hand, means, as the term implies, that the authorities or their agents take the initiative in operating in the market. They do not wait to be approached by would-be buyers or sellers, but themselves bid for, or offer for sale, the foreign currencies, thereby seeking to influence the exchange rates. Passive intervention means that the authorities are on the defensive, and their aim is to retain their position. Active intervention means that they take the offensive with the object of gaining ground. In the case of the former the exchange remains stable, while in the case of the latter it moves in the direction desired by the authorities—assuming, of course, in both instances that the intervention is successful, which is by no means always the case.

This does not mean, however, that passive intervention always aims at maintaining the exchange at the same rate, or that active intervention always aims at changing it. The authorities in charge of the operations may consider it expedient to change the rate at which the exchange is pegged; in other words, to "move the peg". Without departing from their passive attitude, they simply change the rate at which they are prepared to buy or sell. This is sometimes regarded as necessary on grounds of economic policy; the authorities may from time to time change their mind as to the level at which they wish to maintain the exchange. On other occasions, the peg is moved for purely tactical reasons. If an exchange is pegged at a certain rate for too long a period it may create an impression that the authorities mean to keep it there permanently. Although sometimes it is convenient for the authorities to lead the market into this belief, on other occasions it may be against their interest. Unless the peg is changed from time to time, the apparent risk attached to speculating for a rise or fall of the exchange becomes reduced to a minimum; while in the case of currencies on a gold basis, it is equivalent to the margin between gold import and export points, plus the disparity between spot and forward rates, in the case of pegged inconvertible currencies it is practically limited by the extent of the disparity between spot and forward rates. If, however, the peg is moved sometimes, speculators have to face a bigger risk, for, in addition to what they pay for the forward exchange, they may also suffer losses through a change of the spot rate. By occasionally changing the peg, the authorities are in a position to discourage speculation and to prevent the development of a sweeping world-wide movement which, if allowed to develop fully, might get out of control.

It may also give the authorities some satisfaction to "penalise" speculators who underrate the strength of the official resources. This end can, however, be attained much more effectively by active intervention designed to "squeeze" the speculators. Active intervention for that purpose may take place even if the authorities do not aim at bringing about a lasting appreciation or depreciation of their exchange. The existence of a big bull or bear position renders the market vulnerable, and a small dose of intervention may then bring results which are entirely out of proportion to the amount spent in the operation. The authorities allow the exchange rate to return to its previous figure once the campaign is successfully accomplished. The net result is the intimidation of the speculators, and a handsome profit for the authorities at their expense.

The authorities may also take the offensive in a different way. Instead of moving the peg against the speculative trend, or attacking speculators by active intervention, they may pretend to yield to the pressure for a short time, thereby filling speculators with false hopes. Thus, if their object is to prevent an unwanted appreciation of the exchange, instead of attacking bull speculators by lowering the rates they may, at the first stage of their operation, allow the exchange to rise; if their object is to prevent a depreciation of the exchange, instead of attacking bears by raising the rates they at first allow the rates to decline. They thereby give speculators sufficient rope to hang themselves. Almost invariably the speculators fall into the trap. Bull or bear positions will increase, and the exchange will become more sensitive to a well-timed counter-attack. When at the second stage of their operation the authorities intervene the effect is usually spectacular, which would not have been possible if their attack had not been preceded by a tactical retreat. By applying this method, the authorities can teach speculation a lesson which is likely to be remembered for some time. Its application is not, however, without dangers; for it is easier to start an avalanche than to check it. The speculative movement which they themselves have encouraged may easily attain sweeping dimensions, and the authorities may find it difficult to regain control of the market.

The method just described was applied systematically and with success by the Bank of Italy during the period 1931–1932. In addition to pegging the lira slightly under par, thereby increasing the risk of bear speculation, the Italian authorities have descended from time to time into the arena by active intervention. Their attack was usually preceded by a tactical retreat as described above, which was followed by a swift bear-squeezing campaign. The reason why the Italian authorities have an exceptionally good chance of success in these occasional raids upon speculators is that they hold an exceptionally tight grip over the lira resources. Thanks to the disciplined attitude of Italian banks, due in part to the corporative system and in part to the "heavy hand" of dictatorship, the authorities can always prevent speculators from carrying their short position with the aid of lire borrowed from Italian banks. As a result, if the official operations in the foreign exchange market after the tactical retreat bring about a scarcity of lire, speculators have no choice but to cover at a loss.

This method can be applied much more effectively against a bear campaign than against a bull campaign. For it is much easier to carry a bull position than a bear position. If bull speculators have adequate resources to carry their position they need not necessarily become frightened into liquidating by a relapse of the exchange. On the other hand, as is shown by the Italian example, bears may be forced into closing their accounts and cutting their losses at a most inopportune moment.

We have seen in the historical survey in this book that during the war the intervention of the British Government through the intermediary of J. P. Morgan & Co. was entirely passive. There was no attempt to employ any such subtle devices as are described above. The authorities confined themselves to buying an unlimited amount of sterling at a fixed rate. On the other hand the Bank of France practised active intervention at times, and so did the Reichsbank. In the later stages of the war, when the peseta and other neutral currencies underwent a marked appreciation, the British, French, and American authorities intervened actively from time to time in Spain and other neutral markets. During the period of post-war inflation in Germany, the Reichsbank repeatedly attempted to check the depreciation of the mark with the aid of active intervention. It was not until 1923–1924 that its efforts were successful. French intervention between 1924 and 1926 was essentially active, as we have seen above. When in 1931 the British authorities resumed intervention it was at first entirely passive. In 1932 and 1933, however, the British authorities repeatedly took the offensive, though most of the time their intervention consisted mainly of pegging sterling and moving the peg whenever necessary. The intervention on the part of the American authorities in defence of the dollar between 1931 and 1933 was invariably passive. Its sole aim was to prevent a depreciation of the dollar beyond gold points pending the shipment of an adequate amount of gold. The intervention of the Italian authorities was passive during the war, but was alternately passive and active in various periods after the war and during the crisis. Intervention on the part of the Japanese authorities, through the Yokohama Specie Bank, was all the time essentially passive; it was simply the continuation of the normal system by which the operations of the Yokohama Specie Bank supplemented the working of the gold standard.

The success of official intervention aiming at preventing a depreciation depends largely upon the resources at the disposal of the authorities and the strength of the genuine non-speculative factors that oppose them. Nevertheless, the skill with which the operations are handled tends to influence the outcome of the fight to no slight extent. If the resources of the authorities in gold and foreign balances are in excess of the amount of potential genuine demand, then their task is comparatively simple. In that case they may regard the activities of bear speculation with equanimity. No matter how powerful the bear movement is, sooner or later the short positions will have to be covered. If, however, the gold and foreign exchange supplies of the authorities are inferior to the potential genuine demand, then the deficiency has to be made

good by skilful operations. In the first place, the enemy
should not be allowed to realise the weakness of the
defence. In this respect, the British authorities committed a grave error by publishing the figures of the
Macmillan Report at a most inopportune moment. It
is true that the relative weakness of the gold reserve
was a matter of public knowledge. Nobody had, however, any idea of the immense strength of the potential
genuine adverse factors. It was generally believed that
London's external short-term assets and liabilities
more or less balanced each other. Much to the surprise
of even the best-informed banking circles, the Macmillan Report made the astounding disclosure that,
while London's short-term foreign liabilities were over
£400 millions, her short-term assets abroad amounted
to just over £150 millions, a great part of which was
known to be hopelessly frozen. The amount of uncovered short-term liabilities were thus well over £300
millions. Had this fact been kept secret, the conclusion
of the Franco-American credit of £50 millions might
have impressed the market. After the publication of
the Macmillan Report, however, that amount was
regarded as a drop in the ocean.

The weakness of sterling's defences was made even
more evident by the method by which the inadequate
resources were handled. It was the proper policy for
the authorities to do their utmost to disguise their
foreign exchange operations as far as possible. This is,
indeed, an extremely difficult task. Foreign exchange
dealers and brokers are extremely shrewd and are not
easily misled. There are several signs from which they
can infer, with a reasonable degree of accuracy, the
presence of official operations. It does not escape their
attention if they come across the same names too

frequently, and for large amounts, on the same day, especially if in the ordinary course of business the turnover of the banks in question is relatively small. Apart from this, there is usually something in the attitude of those in charge of the official operations that gives them away. Generally speaking, there is much less bargaining about the rate if the deal is done on official account. While banks buying exchange on their own account, or on account of their customers, fight for every fraction of a cent, when they operate on account of the authorities they do not worry about differences of $\frac{1}{4}$ cent or more. Apart from this, some dealers suggest that there is something in the whole attitude of those in charge of the "control", who are conscious of their own importance and cannot always disguise this feeling, that gives the game away. In any case, experienced dealers have developed an instinct for discriminating between commercial and official operations even if there is no concrete clue to help them. Just as the experienced banker can usually spot the finance bill amongst commercial bills, and can usually sense the speculative buying order for securities or currencies, he can also point out, with a reasonable degree of accuracy, the existence of official dealings. Thus, even if the control is operated with the utmost skill, it is difficult to deceive the market. This is no reason, however, for omitting to make an attempt to conceal official operations.

As the British resources in August 1931 were insufficient, it was particularly important to conceal the extent to which they were being drawn upon. Instead of aiming at this, the authorities carried out their operations in a way which made them obvious enough for the least alert of dealers to notice them. They made the mistake of putting two medium-sized banks in charge of the defence of sterling; one of them operated the dollar exchange and the other the French franc. The market soon became aware that the volume of the operations of these two banks was a multiple of their normal turnover, and rightly concluded that they were acting on behalf of the authorities. As a result, it was easy for dealers, by comparing notes as to the amount of their dealings with these banks, to form an idea as to the extent to which the official resources were being used up. It took little time for the information to spread outside the bounds of London, and before long the banking centres of Paris, New York, Amsterdam, etc., were also fully acquainted with the position. This is by no means a reflection upon the skill with which the two banks in question operated. None but the largest banks with a considerable turnover of their own could have disguised to any appreciable extent the official operations. This was subsequently realised by the authorities and, towards the end of August, a number of leading banks were put in charge. Even then the market had a vague idea that the foreign exchange resources were being drawn upon. The extent of the operations was not, however, accurately realised, and the announcement made on September 20, 1931, that the proceeds of the second Franco-American credit had been exhausted, came as an almost complete surprise to most dealers. It would have been decidedly to the advantage of the authorities if they had put the clearing banks in charge of the control from the very beginning.

The above criticism of the authorities for failing adequately to disguise their operations does not mean that it is always desirable, in order to ensure success, to conceal the fact that intervention is taking place. On

the contrary, on some occasions it suits the purpose of
the authorities to come into the open, as publicity
assists them in their task. This was the case with M.
Poincaré's memorable bear-squeezing campaign in
1924. Everybody in the market knew which banks were
in charge of the official support. Speculators all over
the world watched the operation of these banks with
keen interest, and the market followed their lead; as a
result, the effect of the official operations was considerably increased.

There are several reasons why the French authorities
were right in pursuing the method of open support in
1924, while the British authorities were wrong in pursuing the same method in 1931:

(1) In 1924 nobody knew the strength of the resources upon which the French operations were based,
nor the strength of the forces opposed to the authorities; in 1931 the market was aware of the limits of the
resources of the British authorities, and had a fairly
good idea as to the strength of the potential pressure.

(2) While in 1924 the opponents whom the French
authorities had to deal with were mainly speculators
who could easily be intimidated by a show of strength,
in 1931 the British authorities had to deal mainly with
foreign holders of sterling balances.

(3) In 1924 nobody knew to what rate the French
authorities wanted the franc to appreciate; in 1931, on
the other hand, the aim of the British authorities was
obviously to maintain sterling above gold export point.

(4) In 1924 the French authorities took the offensive,
and for that purpose publicity was helpful; while in
1931 British authorities were on the defensive, and for
that purpose publicity was harmful.

This last point is of particular importance. In case

of active support the evidence of official transactions
in the market may be interpreted as a sign of strength,
while in case of passive support it is always a sign of
weakness. It is impossible for the authorities, engaged
in active intervention, to squeeze the bears without
spending a certain amount of their resources. On the
other hand, if the authorities merely aim at defending
the stability of the exchange, and to that end have to
spend part of their resources, it shows that the natural
tendency of the exchange would be in a downward
direction, and that it is being bolstered up artificially.

It is, of course, possible to combine open and disguised support. The French authorities repeatedly
resorted to this method between 1924 and 1926. On
certain occasions the banks which were known to be
acting as agents for the authorities were operating in
one direction, while the authorities were at the same
time operating also the opposite way, through the
intermediary of banks whose connection with official
quarters was not known to the market. Thus, if the
authorities wanted to support the franc without using
up their foreign exchange resources, the banks which
at the time were known to be in charge of the official
operations were selling foreign currencies, giving thereby a lead to the market, while at the same time some
other bank was replenishing the supply of the authorities unobserved. In 1931 it was impossible for the
British authorities to apply this method, even if they
had been sufficiently subtle to do so, for the market did
not follow the lead of the banks in charge of official
transactions, and there was thus no opportunity for
replenishing the dwindling official supply of dollars and
francs. Possibly during the second half of 1932 our

authorities might have resorted to this method, as conditions were then decidedly more in their favour.

During the summer of 1932, the necessity for supporting sterling arose once again, though to a much smaller extent than a year before. The situation was totally different from that of 1931. Our general position had become much stronger, and our authorities were known to have acquired substantial reserves available for the support of sterling. In such circumstances it was no longer necessary to conceal supporting operations; on the contrary, it would have been to the advantage of the authorities to benefit by the psychological effect of their operations. For, whenever dealers assumed that the control was in the market, they usually operated in the same direction, thereby accentuating the effect of the official intervention. A comparatively small amount of buying of sterling on the part of the authorities was sufficient to arrest the decline, and even to bring about a rise in the rate. Strangely enough, our authorities did not take advantage of this situation. Instead of operating with wide publicity, they employed considerable skill for concealing the transactions. Day after day they changed the banks through which they operated, and very often by the time the market identified the bank or banks which at the moment enjoyed the passing favour of the great, the control was already being transferred to another bank. The authorities even went so far as to arrange the support of sterling in Paris or New York so as to disguise their operations. In doing so, they diverted foreign exchange business from London to other centres; apparently they were so anxious to conceal their operations that they were prepared thus to sacrifice the legitimate interests of the London market.

Although they did not altogether succeed in attaining their end—especially as secrets leak out abroad much more easily than in this country—they did succeed in confusing the dealers; very frequently the market was in doubt whether or not the control was operating. Had these tactics been pursued in the summer of 1931 it would have been very useful. A year later, however, secrecy was disadvantageous. Owing to the absence of adequate publicity, the authorities had to use up much larger amounts of their resources to attain the same result. Thus, they have pursued both the tactics of publicity and of secrecy at the wrong time.

Earlier in this chapter reference was made to the practice of moving the peg temporarily from the figure where the authorities want to maintain the exchange. If it is moved in accordance with the tendency of the speculative pressure—that is, if it is raised when there is a buying pressure or lowered when there is a selling pressure—the object is to encourage speculators so as to be able to squeeze them all the better. If it is moved against the tendency of speculative pressure, the object is to discourage speculators by a display of strength. This latter device was attempted by our authorities during the summer of 1931, when, in order to lead the market into the belief that the situation was well in hand, the peg of the dollar and the franc was raised above gold export point. Owing to the circumstances of the operations, however, these tactics deceived nobody. The same tactics were repeated more successfully on a small scale on various occasions during the summer and early autumn of 1932.

Another method attempted for the same purpose in 1931 was the artificial reduction of the discount on forward sterling. Possibly the object of this measure was to raise forward sterling above gold export point. Doubtless, if the forward rate for a currency is below gold export point it creates a bad impression. This cannot, however, be avoided by raising it above gold export point if the market is aware that the rise is purely artificial. In 1931 these tactics failed to produce a favourable psychological effect, while the material effect was decidedly harmful. It encouraged the withdrawal of funds as well as bear speculation in sterling. The reduction of the premium on forward dollars and francs made it cheaper for foreign holders of sterling time deposits to sell their holding forward. The importance of this factor should not, however, be exaggerated. As foreign holders of sterling lost confidence in the stability of that currency they hastened to safeguard themselves against the risk; considerations of interest rate or of the cost of covering the forward exchange ceased to play any important part in their decision. But the reduction of the cost of covering the forward exchange below the difference between interest rates in London and in foreign centres encouraged forward selling even on the part of those who did not particularly distrust the stability of sterling. Also, the extent to which the policy of the authorities tended to encourage speculation against sterling was by no means inconsiderable. By raising forward rates above gold points, the authorities practically removed the risk attached to bear speculation in sterling. In theory, speculators run the risk of an appreciation of sterling to gold import point. In practice, however, on the eve of the seasonal autumn pressure, there was no such risk, for even in normal years sterling is usually in the vicinity of gold point between the end of August and the end of December. Had forward sterling been allowed to remain under gold export point it might have deterred many speculators. As it was, they stood a chance of making a big profit without having to take even a negligible risk.

The Central Banks of other countries apparently learnt at the expense of the British authorities, and when it was their turn to defend their currencies, they adopted a totally different policy. On several occasions, towards the end of 1931 and in 1932, when, in consequence of the withdrawal of foreign balances and speculative activities, the dollar, the guilder, and the Belgian franc depreciated to the vicinity of their gold export points, the authorities allowed the forward exchanges to depreciate well below gold export point. The Dutch authorities went even further, and artificially widened the discount rate on forward guilders. While reasonable forward rates were quoted for *bona fide* commercial requirements, the rates quoted for speculative purposes were bordering on the prohibitive. The Dutch authorities thus increased the expense of covering the exchange risk attached to speculative selling of guilders. Although it would be an exaggeration to suggest that the maintenance of the stability of the guilder was due to this policy, it had undoubtedly a certain share in preventing the development of a world-wide wave of speculation against the guilder.

It is a highly controversial question whether Central Banks should take an active interest in forward exchange or whether they should confine their intervention to the spot market. In this respect, the general view has changed considerably during the last few years. Before the financial crisis there was a strong current in favour of Central Banks taking an active interest in the forward exchange market, not necessarily in order to stabilise the exchange, but in order to improve ordinary facilities. It was even proposed that the Bank for International Settlements should become a clearing house for forward exchange transactions. This scheme was, however, rejected; nor were the suggestions that Central Banks should take an increased interest in the forward exchange market ever followed. We have seen that, during the crisis, the Bank of England operated in forward exchange to the same extent as in spot exchange. The Federal Reserve authorities and the National Bank of Belgium, however, while supporting the spot exchange, remained strictly neutral in the forward market. The Bank of England, too, discontinued its operations in forward exchange after the suspension of the gold standard, and its intervention during 1932 confined itself to the spot market. When in March 1932 they tried to prevent an unwanted rise of sterling, they bought up the spot dollars and francs thrown on the market, but did not touch the forward currencies. As a result, the forward dollar rate went to a discount equivalent to 4 to 5 per cent per annum at the beginning of March, and this might have discouraged bull speculation, but for the fact that the market anticipated a big rise. A premium of 4 to 5 per cent per annum on forward sterling was considered, therefore, a fair risk.

In consequence of the failure of the efforts to maintain sterling in the vicinity of 3·50 early in 1932, there was some criticism of this method, which was regarded by some experts as being largely responsible for the victory of bull speculation in its struggle against the authorities. In reality, the failure to keep sterling down was not due to any technical flaw in the method of intervention, but to the fact that the authorities fixed a comparatively low limit for the amount of foreign exchanges they were prepared to buy. The contention that, had the control been extended over the forward exchange market, the unwanted rise of sterling might have been averted, is based on the argument that the wide premium on forward sterling encouraged arbitrageurs to buy spot sterling and invest it in Treasury bills. In doing so, foreign banks were able to secure a yield of $7\frac{1}{2}$ per cent per annum, without taking any exchange risk. Undoubtedly, such operations increased the demand for spot sterling to no slight extent, and it is therefore correct to say that, but for the wide premium on forward sterling, the amount of spot exchanges the authorities were compelled to take up would have been much smaller. On the other hand, in order to keep down the premium on forward sterling, they would have had to buy substantial amounts of forward exchange. Their limit would therefore have been reached about the same time as it actually was reached, or possibly even sooner. While on the one hand the demand for spot sterling for interest arbitrage was a burden on the authorities, the covering of these operations by selling forward sterling relieved the authorities to exactly the same extent. Moreover, had the premium on forward sterling been kept artificially low by official intervention in the forward exchange market, it would have tended to encourage bull speculation in sterling, so that the chances are that the total buying pressure on sterling would have been even stronger.

It is true that the discouraging effect of a wide premium on forward sterling upon speculation was neutralised by the gradual rise in the spot rate which was allowed to take place even before the authorities definitely yielded to the buying pressure on March 8, 1932. As sterling rose point by point every day, speculators were not deterred from running up bear positions by the cost of the forward operations, amounting to three to four points for three months. In this respect, the authorities are open to criticism. Had they rigidly maintained the spot rate for some time, possibly it might have discouraged speculators from risking the loss of these three or four points. But here again, the main question was not one of tactics but of policy. The prolonged defence of the spot rate against a rise might have necessitated the purchase of larger amounts of foreign exchange than the authorities were prepared to buy. The success of their endeavours to prevent a rise depended mainly upon their willingness to buy large amounts, and only to a small extent upon the methods by which the operations were managed.

Another question to be examined is whether the exchange should be pegged against one or several currencies. Before the crisis, it was a general rule in every country where intervention was practised to peg the exchange against one currency, which was usually either sterling or the dollar. During the sterling crisis of 1931, the British authorities endeavoured to peg sterling in relation to both dollar and franc. As the bulk of the demand for foreign currencies was for dollars, the main effort had to be focussed upon the sterling-dollar rate, and the sterling-franc rate was adjusted to that rate in accordance with requirements. No attempt was, however, made to peg sterling in relation to other gold currencies. As a result of this omission, the Dutch guilder rate declined below gold export point in September 1931, and the ensuing outflow of gold from London to Amsterdam provided the final blow that brought about the collapse of the pound. It would have been decidedly better to make the defence of sterling watertight in every direction.

This does not, however, mean that it is advisable, as a general rule, to peg an exchange in relation to several other currencies. Amidst the unsettled international financial conditions such a task would be beyond the capacity of almost any country. For, if A is made equal both to B and C, then B and C have to be made equal to one another. If sterling were to be rigidly pegged in relation to both dollar and franc, this would amount to the pegging of the dollar and the franc in relation to one another. As a result, whenever either of the two currencies tended to develop weakness, this country would support it automatically. If the arrangement were to be extended to all gold currencies, the Bank of England would assume the duties of Atlas in carrying the burden of the whole universe. A flight from any of the gold currencies would then be neutralised by the arrangement which would maintain all gold currencies at par—or at any rate within their gold points. It is a matter of opinion whether this country could or should perform such a service. While many people would consider it desirable to eliminate the danger of the depreciation of the few currencies which are still on an effective gold basis, it is questionable whether it would be wise to enable the countries concerned to have an unbalanced budget without running the risk of paying the penalty for it, through a depreciation of their currencies. It is equally open to argument whether it is wise to interfere with the working of the gold standard between the countries that are still on a gold basis.

From the point of view of preventing an unwanted

rise it is clearly superfluous to peg sterling in relation
to two or more currencies. Unilateral pegging to one of
the two principal gold currencies is sufficient. Nor is it
necessary to peg sterling always in relation to the same
currency. Early in 1932 our authorities pursued the
policy of pegging sterling in relation to the dollar. They
were buyers of any amounts of dollars that were offered
at the rate at which sterling happened to be pegged.
As a result, the American authorities were enabled to
regard the flight from the dollar with comparative
equanimity, since a great part of the dollars thrown on
the market was bought up by the British authorities,
and the exceedingly valuable support thus provided
made it less imperative for the United States to balance
her budget and put her house in order generally. As
the primary object of the operations was not to save
the dollar, but to prevent a rise of sterling, this could
have been attained by pegging sterling to the franc.
In fact, our authorities switched over on several occasions from June 1932 onward, from the dollar to the
franc, but the general rule remained, nevertheless, to
peg sterling in relation to the weaker of the two currencies. At the beginning of 1933, however, they re-
versed their policy and began to peg sterling to the
stronger of the two major gold currencies. They
refrained from bolstering up the dollar with their purchases during the crisis of February and March 1933.
Had they not changed their policy possibly they might
have prevented the suspension of the gold standard in
the United States for a while, but as it was bound to
take place eventually they would have incurred heavy
ultimate losses on the huge dollar balance they would
have accumulated in the meantime.

This brings us to the question of the profits and

losses brought about by intervention. Although considerations of profit and loss cannot be altogether disregarded, they ought to occupy a secondary place when judging the results of intervention. Desirable as it is to produce a windfall to the Exchequer in the form of profits on official foreign exchange operations, it is much more important that intervention should achieve its primary object of maintaining the currency at the level desired. If this result can be combined with earning a good profit on those operations it is all the better, but the authorities should not be influenced in their policy to an unduly great extent by their desire for popular applause on account of the profit earned on their operations. If the main object of a foreign exchange policy can only be obtained at the cost of losses, the amounts lost are well spent.

Throughout this chapter, the technique adopted by the British authorities in their intervention has been subject to much criticism. In all fairness it must be admitted that, by the end of 1932, they had acquired a praiseworthy skill in managing the exchange. Since then any errors committed were mostly errors of policy, not of tactics. The Exchange Equalisation Fund has become a formidable power in the market, and its prestige is due to the technical skill with which it operated at least as much as to the magnitude of its resources.

CHAPTER X

THE ECONOMICS OF EXCHANGE RESTRICTIONS

IT may be stated without fear of contradiction that exchange restrictions are the best-hated method of Exchange Control, and indeed amongst the best-hated Government measures of interference in the eyes of the majority of expert and inexpert opinion. Compared with them intervention is almost popular. There is, in fact, a considerable difference between these two methods of Exchange Control. Intervention consists of official exchange operations in the desired direction. Restrictions consist of the prevention of private exchange operations in an undesirable direction. Intervention, while interfering with natural tendencies in the exchanges, does not interfere with the freedom of exchange operations. In the eyes of purists it may offend the laws of economic science as conceived in the nineteenth century, but it does not offend the much more fundamental laws of human nature, which resents any restriction of freedom. On the other hand, exchange restrictions violate both the abstract laws of economic science by which tendencies in exchanges should be allowed to take care of themselves, and the feelings of a large part of the public, jealous for the safeguarding of its traditional freedom of action. It is thus no wonder that exchange restrictions are subject to incomparably more frequent and more violent attacks than intervention. Unfortunately by far the greater part of criticism assumes the form of abusive denunciation in a tone bordering on hysteria, without any constructive spirit behind it.

Admittedly it would be difficult to justify exchange restrictions in face of the criticisms levelled against it. The majority of these criticisms may be classed under three headings:

(1) Exchange restrictions tend to maintain the exchanges at an abnormal level.

(2) They have a highly damaging effect on international trade.

(3) They are utterly inefficient and impossible to enforce.

The question of bolstering up the exchange at an abnormal level was dealt with at some length in the last three chapters. We have said that no lasting result can as a rule be achieved against fundamental tendencies, but that interference against speculative and seasonal fluctuations is possible and desirable. When judging the *raison d'être* of exchange restrictions we have to examine how far the tendencies against which they are directed are normal and fundamental. We have seen in Chapter II. that the object of exchange restrictions may be:

(1) To prevent speculation.

(2) To prevent an outflow of capital.

(3) To control private holdings of foreign currencies.

(4) To prevent the transfer of foreign debt payments.

(5) To prevent excessive imports.

There can be no doubt that speculation is not a fundamental factor, and that to fight against it is not to prevent, but to safeguard, the normal working of fundamental tendencies. It is true that, in theory, speculation unsupported by fundamental tendencies is bound to collapse. In practice, however, a persistent speculative movement is fully capable of making changes in fundamental tendencies themselves. Thus, if speculation is capable of maintaining a currency for some time above or below its economic parities, the chances are that these economic parities will to some extent tend to adjust themselves to the abnormal exchange rates. For this reason the principle of counteracting speculation by fair means or foul is justified even from the standpoint of economic purism. It is true that intervention is a much more suitable weapon than restrictions against speculation. As, however, the latter can supplement and assist intervention, they can fulfil a useful rôle in the campaign against speculation.

International capital movements constitute a most powerful abnormal factor interfering with the working of fundamental economic tendencies. They are apt, to a much higher degree than speculation, to bring about lasting changes in fundamental factors. If the authorities endeavour to prevent abnormal capital movements from affecting the exchanges, they assist in the working of normal tendencies, instead of obstructing them. The trouble is, in the case of both speculation and capital movements, that they very often express normal and fundamental tendencies, and that it is most difficult to discriminate between such justified movements and abnormal and unjustified movements. As exchange restrictions are applied indiscriminately against every kind of speculative and capital movement, they very often interfere with the working of genuine fundamental tendencies.

The measures restricting private holdings in foreign countries are complementary to measures against capital movements. Whether or not we consider them justifiable depends upon our conception of the rights of the State towards individuals. In times of emergency it is undoubtedly justifiable for the State to seize foreign assets held by individuals, for the sake of public interest. The measures compelling the surrender of dollar bonds during the war is an example of such justified action. The question is whether an economic crisis may be regarded in the same light as the state of emergency created by a war. Undoubtedly the difference is merely one of degree, and it is impossible to lay down a hard and fast rule as to when the emergency is sufficiently grave to justify Government intervention of this nature.

Whether or not exchange restrictions aiming at the prevention of transfers on account of interest and principle of foreign debts are justified depends on a totally different set of considerations. The problem can best be approached by comparing the position of the debtor country with that of an individual debtor. The moment a private debtor realises that he is unable to meet all his liabilities, it is his duty to suspend payments so as to make it possible that all debtors should obtain a due proportion of his assets, instead of following the rule of "first come first served". The same is true concerning a debtor country. The moment its Government realises that there is a drain on its assets with which it is unable to cope, in all fairness to all foreign creditors it ought to place restrictions upon the transfer of the service of foreign debt. Such restrictions are fully justified provided that they are not used for the purpose of repaying part of the debt well under par. Unfortunately there were many instances of such abuses during the last few years, the most conspicuous being the case of Germany. Restrictions upon debt payments naturally brought about a depreciation of the debt, and many debtors took advantage of this situation by repaying part of their debts at a low price, with the connivance of the authorities.

The most unpopular type of exchange restrictions is that aiming at the reduction of imports. They are denounced as an abnormal interference with the working of trade balances which, in the opinion of liberal economists, should be allowed to look after themselves. Our judgment whether such restrictions are justified depends largely upon our attitude in the free trade *versus* protection controversy. If we admit the Government's right to reduce imports artificially, it remains to be decided whether exchange restrictions are a more appropriate means than tariffs, quotas, or embargoes on certain imports.

The second set of objections to exchange restrictions is based upon its injurious effect on trade. It is beyond doubt that the shrinkage in the volume of international trade since 1931 was largely due to exchange restrictions. To some extent, however, one man's poison has proved in many cases to be another man's meat. While exchange restrictions reduced international trade, they stimulated to some extent internal trade in various countries. From the point of view of stimulating home trade at the expense of foreign trade, exchange restrictions compare, however, unfavourably with protective tariffs. The latter are introduced as part of the declared policy of the Government and their introduction encourages capital investment in the protected spheres. Exchange restrictions, on the other hand, are always regarded as temporary emergency measures, and it is a risky undertaking to build up industries with costly plant under the shelter of such temporary protection. Notwithstanding this, a number of industrial enterprises were established all over the world as a result of exchange restrictions, in the hope that those restrictions would last long enough to give a chance for the new enterprises to consolidate themselves. It is, moreover, hoped that once the new industries are established they will obtain permanent protection after the removal of exchange restrictions.

The adverse effect of exchange restrictions on trade was mitigated to no slight extent by the establishment of Exchange Clearing, and also by a number of barter arrangements between various countries. These arrangements will be dealt with in later chapters. Here it is sufficient to point out that with the aid of such arrangements it is possible to reduce considerably the evil effect of exchange restrictions on international trade.

The third set of objections to exchange restrictions contests their efficiency amongst the methods of exchange restrictions. It is pointed out that all the irksome interference with the freedom of the market is in vain because it does not achieve its object. There are innumerable loopholes through which exchange restrictions can be circumvented. If the pressure against which restrictions are used is powerful and persistent, the odds are heavily against the authorities. The greater the discrepancy between the artificial level maintained by exchange restrictions and the natural level to which the exchange would tend to move in the absence of restrictions, the stronger the temptation to make use of the loopholes. Indeed, in such circumstances exchange restrictions tend to become a penalty on loyalty and a premium on disloyalty. Whenever an exchange is maintained at an artificial level with the aid of exchange restrictions, an unofficial market develops, the quotations of which represent the natural price of the currency concerned. Thus, in practice the exchange will depreciate notwithstanding the restrictions. These criticisms have lost much of their force during the last few years, thanks to the improvement in the methods of restriction. Although a perfectly watertight system of exchange restrictions is yet to be invented, its methods have undoubtedly improved, and in countries where it is applied with intelligence and vigour it is comparatively effective. Evasions have become the exception rather than the rule, and to a great extent restrictions in various countries have achieved their object.

Whether or not we agree with the policy of exchange restrictions, we must admit that there is a strong case against their immediate and unconditional removal. It is only *laissez-faire* fanatics who believe that it is the sacred duty of every Government to restore immediately the full freedom of the foreign exchange market. The more moderate amongst them advocate international action in preference to unilateral decision by individual Governments, but failing the former they prefer the latter to the continuation of restrictions. They honestly and seriously believe that a country could remove exchange restrictions, irrespective of what its neighbours are doing in the matter, and live happily ever after. In reality such a policy would be suicidal for any country which does not possess a considerable gold reserve. The hopes that such an example would be followed immediately by a large number of other countries are negligible. If the example is not followed immediately the result would be, in all probability, a rapid depletion of the gold reserve of the country, followed by a slump in its currency. The experiment would end up by the restoration of restrictions to escape starvation and chaos.

Even if all Governments were to decide unanimously to remove simultaneously all exchange restrictions—a possibility which, in the light of the experience of the London Economic Conference of 1933, may appear to be rather remote—the decision would be a leap in the dark for the financially weaker countries. The removal of exchange restriction will have to be a gradual process and will have to be accompanied by adequate safeguards.

CHAPTER XI

THE TECHNIQUE OF EXCHANGE RESTRICTIONS

THE degree of efficiency of exchange restrictions depends upon a number of factors. As a general rule it may be said that the extent to which exchange restrictions are effective is in inverse ratio to the extent of the freedom allowed for foreign exchange operations. It is only natural that a stricter curtailment of free activity in the foreign exchange market tends to increase the efficiency of the restrictions. There are, however, other considerations which influence the success or otherwise of this form of Exchange Control. Even the most carefully devised legislative measures will remain a dead letter unless they can be enforced through the loyal collaboration of the banks and of the public in general. Failing that, the success of restrictions depends upon the strictness of sanctions against those who try to evade them. If the public and the banks are not law-abiding by nature, fear of heavy penalties in the form of fines, confiscations, and imprisonment may deter them from breaking the law. Generally speaking, it is easier to enforce exchange restrictions in comparatively primitive countries than in the most highly developed countries where there is a multitude of channels available for those who want to circumvent the law.

We have seen in the historical part of this book that the efficiency of exchange restrictions tends to increase in the course of time through experience. Although the mind of the authorities works more slowly than that of the highly subtle and ingenious opponents with whom they have to cope, the chances are that they will gradually succeed in blocking most of the loopholes, at any rate to a sufficient extent to reduce the leakage to relatively insignificant proportions. This end is likely to be achieved not merely by additional legislation but also by the increased efficiency in the application of the existing rules. Three countries at least have reached an advanced stage of development in the system of their Exchange Control. In Russia, the "black bourse" has become a mere shadow of its old self. In Germany there is hardly any evasion without the consent or encouragement of the authorities. In Italy, the unofficial restrictions work, on the whole, efficiently, thanks to the discipline enforced by Signor Mussolini. In most other countries exchange restrictions are still at a less advanced stage, partly because discipline is not enforced to the same extent by the fear of penalties, and partly because the Governments are unwilling to go to extremes in curtailing the freedom of the market.

The extent to which exchange restrictions can be enforced depends also to a large extent upon the resources available for transfer abroad. Such resources are not unlimited provided that the emigration of the nationals is prevented. So long as they have to live in the country concerned they have to retain a certain part of their fortunes. In any case it is impossible to convert more than a fraction of the national wealth into liquid assets suitable for transfer abroad. Once the limit of such liquid resources is approached, the circumvention of restrictions naturally slows down. In the case of Germany, for instance, so much capital had been exported abroad during 1931 and 1932 that in

1933 it was comparatively easy to put a stop to the outflow, as there was relatively little left that could be exported.

The degrees of restriction applied at various times and in various countries are, in the order of their strictness, the following:

(1) Unofficial discouragement of capital export and speculation.

(2) Official prohibition of capital export and speculation applied by the banks.

(3) Prohibition of capital export and speculation applied by the authorities.

(4) Application of the prohibition of export on foreign capital (transfer moratorium).

(5) Allocation of foreign exchanges for importers by permits.

(6) Compulsory surrender of foreign exchanges by exporters.

(7) Compulsory surrender of existing foreign exchange holdings by private interests.

(8) Complete suspension of free dealing.

There are a variety of shades and degrees of unofficial discouragement. It proved to be ineffective whenever it was applied unless it assumed the form of pressure which almost amounted to official restrictions. During the war the authorities in Great Britain, France, Germany, etc., hoped for a long time to attain their end without having to introduce official restrictions, but by 1918 moral pressure had to be replaced everywhere by legal rules. In 1931, after the suspension of the gold standard, it was attempted to apply self-imposed exchange restrictions, but after a few days legal measures had to be taken. In Italy exchange restrictions are in theory unofficial, but in practice those who are caught violating them are treated as the enemies of the public interest even in the absence of any specific legislation. Generally speaking, unofficial exchange restrictions constitute a premium on disloyalty and are therefore grossly unfair to the law-abiding section of the public and of the banking community.

Whenever exchange restrictions were in force in Great Britain the banks were placed in charge of their execution. During the war, as well as in 1931–1932, it was left to the discretion of the banks to decide whether or not any particular proposed transaction aimed at violating the rules. They had to use their own judgment to decide whether any demand for foreign exchanges was for genuine commercial or financial requirements or whether it aimed at the export of capital. There was no official supervision of their activities, as they enjoyed the confidence of the authorities. The same system was adopted at one time or other by several other countries with a varying degree of success. Provided that the banks are loyal they are unquestionably in a better position to judge the genuine character of transactions than any official organisation. After all, they have been dealing with their clients for years and know a great deal about the nature of their requirements in foreign exchanges. On the other hand, if all banks are not equally loyal those determined to enforce the law are placed at a disadvantage as they stand to lose some of their customers. They are frequently confronted with dilemmas of divided allegiance. It is often difficult for them to ascertain whether the nationals buying foreign currencies or the foreign banks asking for credits in the national currency do not aim at violating the law. In the absence of adequate arrangements for pooling information they are unable to check the activities of those customers who work with several banks.

From this point of view the system by which the restrictions, though operated by the banks, are subject to official supervision certainly constitutes an improvement from the point of view of efficiency. This system was adopted by the United States during the last year of the war, as well as in 1933 after the suspension of the gold standard. Although in many ways this system compares favourably with the previous one, it is not without disadvantages. It relieves the banks, to a great extent, of the responsibility for evasion. While under the previous system they fulfilled the rôle of Government representatives, under this system they are more at liberty to support the interests of their customers against those of the Government, since the latter's interests are to be safeguarded by the inspector placed in charge of restrictions.

The milder forms of exchange restrictions are directed solely against the export of capital by nationals or by foreign residents in the country. Foreigners are only affected by the restrictions aiming at discouraging bear speculation in the national currency, but are at liberty to withdraw any capital they possess. It is this principle which was enforced in the Anglo-Saxon countries and in Japan. On the Continent and in Latin America, on the other hand, no discrimination has been made in favour of foreign capital. During and after the war foreigners owning capital in these countries were subject to exactly the same regulations as nationals. Since the beginning of the financial crisis in 1931 foreign capital was further affected, in a large number of countries, by various forms and degrees of transfer

moratoria. The technicalities of the situation created
by such restrictions will be dealt with in the next chapter. We shall see that transfer moratoria have led to
the creation of a variety of blocked currencies, the
marketing of which partly defeated the object of the
restrictions.

The prohibition of the purchase of foreign exchanges
by those desirous of transferring their capital abroad
is by no means the only way of restricting capital outflow. The same end is served also by an embargo on the
export of securities, notes and gold. In addition, the
import of securities and of notes is also often subject to
restrictions. In particular, the import of notes is often
subject to restrictions so as to discourage the export
of notes for the purpose of transferring capital. It is by
no means easy to supervise the frontiers sufficiently to
prevent the export of notes, but if difficulties are made
in the way of making use of the notes thus exported
for payment in the country concerned, foreign banks
may be unwilling to buy large amounts. The restriction
on the import of securities on foreign account is
directed against repayment of foreign debt rather than
capital transfer. The restrictions on speculation assume
the form of prohibition of the sale of foreign currencies
for non-commercial requirements and of the granting
of overdrafts to foreigners. Occasionally, special restrictions are imposed upon forward exchange dealing in
general.

The types of exchange restrictions dealt with so far
were concerned only with capital movements and
speculative activities. They did not aim at interfering
with foreign exchange operations for imports, exports,
and other normal commercial activities. The next
degree is when the authorities reserve the right to allot

the foreign exchanges required by importers, who have to produce a permit in order to obtain the currencies they need. In many cases this is a mere matter of form, and its object is solely to prevent the purchase of currencies for speculation or capital export. More frequently, however, the authorities aim at a reduction of imports in general, or certain types of imports in particular. This can be achieved either by delaying the granting of permits until, in the opinion of the authorities, the supply of foreign exchanges is sufficient to cover the requirements, or by the refusal of permits for certain types of imports, or by the fixing of quotas for the allotment of permits. Discrimination is sometimes made according to the currency claimed. It is comparatively easy to enforce restrictions of this kind through the co-operation between the currency authorities and customs authorities.

The next stage in advanced exchange restrictions is the compulsory surrender of foreign currencies by exporters. This rule is rather more difficult to enforce than the restriction on exchanges for importers. There are many ways by which exporters are able to leave the proceeds of their exports abroad. In many cases the authorities conclude a compromise by which they are satisfied if exporters surrender a certain percentage of their currencies and use the rest for their own import requirements.

A still stricter form of restriction is reached when holders of foreign balances or investments are compelled to surrender their holdings. Such measures were applied in Great Britain during the war as far as dollar securities were concerned. They are being applied in Germany with draconian rigour. Any German citizen who fails to declare and surrender his foreign currencies is liable to prosecution for "economic treason", the punishment for which is long-term imprisonment and confiscation of property. A milder form of the same restriction exists in Japan, where everybody has to declare his foreign assets, though nobody has so far been called upon to surrender them. It is extremely difficult for the authorities of any country to enforce such restrictions. There are innumerable ways by which holdings of foreign assets can be disguised, and in the absence of any co-operation between the authorities of various countries it is difficult to trace such assets and entirely impossible to seize them. In so far as they are managed by banks abroad the secrets of customers are jealously safeguarded. Provisions are sometimes made to avoid any correspondence on the subject of the accounts in question, for fear that the telegrams or letters might be intercepted. In certain countries, particularly in Switzerland, the banks specialise in such secret accounts, which often bear no name but merely a password so as to safeguard their owners against espionage and leakage of information. In the circumstances it may be said that, generally speaking, this type of exchange restriction is the most ineffective.

The most extreme form of exchange restriction consists of a complete suppression of free dealings in exchanges. This can be achieved by the concentration of all foreign exchange business in the hands of the Central Bank or other authority appointed for the task. Under such a system importers can only buy foreign currencies from the authorities and exporters are compelled to sell their foreign currencies to the authorities. A somewhat milder application of the same system is that in which a certain number of banks are appointed to act as agents for the authorities and to buy and sell exchanges on their behalf on a commission basis. In substance this system differs but little from a complete monopoly of exchange operations by the authorities. Needless to say, such monopoly exists only in law and not in fact, for in every country where it is applied there is a "black bourse" for illicit dealings. No country has yet succeeded in suppressing the "black bourse" completely, though in some countries its significance has been reduced considerably. In other countries, on the other hand, the Government, recognising its inability to suppress the "black bourse", restored a certain degree of free dealing under licence. In Austria, for instance, the exchange rates prevailing in the former "black bourse" have been recognised as the official rates, and importers and exporters possessing the National Bank's permit are at liberty to buy and sell currencies in the open market.

CHAPTER XII

BLOCKED ACCOUNTS

ONE of the unexpected results of the economic crisis has been the extension of the vocabulary of every language. Before 1931 terms such as "Standstill Agreement", "Blocked Currencies", "Additional Exports", "Exchange Clearing", etc., were unknown even to the financial experts, while to-day they are household words in financial and business communities, and even the general public uses them freely. The system of blocked accounts is amongst the innovations which have resulted in the extension of our vocabulary. It is a new type of exchange restriction which was not applied anywhere until 1931. Since then it has been widely adopted by a large number of countries in Europe and in Latin America. It originated as a result of the desire of a number of countries to maintain the stability of their currencies in face of transfer difficulties. To that end it has been found that transfer restrictions by themselves are not sufficient. For even the most efficient system of exchange restrictions has loopholes, and is thereby unable to prevent the transfer of funds abroad entirely. The idea of the blocked currency system is to supplement transfer restrictions by reducing the amount of funds available for transfer abroad. It does not in any way affect the ability of nationals of the country concerned to export their capital. It prevents foreigners, however, from withdrawing their funds, unless they are prepared to cut a loss by selling their blocked currencies at a heavy discount.

Those who have claims against foreign countries, whether through commercial or financial transactions or through being holders of the bonds of the country concerned, have been affected by the crisis in a twofold way. First, the insolvency of a number of foreign debtors has made it difficult for them to collect their claims. Secondly, the currency situation in the debtors' countries has made it difficult for the debtors to make the necessary exchange transfers for the settlement of their debts. The blocked currency system aims at enabling the solvent debtors to make payment in their own national currencies without having to make any exchange transfers.

An object of the blocked currency system is to safeguard the interests of solvent debtors against the consequences of a currency depreciation. If they are prevented by exchange restrictions from meeting their foreign liabilities, they are exposed to the risk that, as a result of a depreciation of the national currency, the burden of their debts in terms of that national currency may increase. To avert such a risk—the mere threat of which might affect the solvency of firms with foreign debts—the Government of some debtor country authorised individual debtors to settle their debts through the payment of the sum owed into a special "blocked account" in national currency. This is, of course, equivalent to empowering the debtors to break their contracts, since the latter provide for payment in some foreign currency. While exchange restrictions and transfer moratoria merely prevent the debtor provisionally from discharging his foreign debts, the measures concerning payments into blocked accounts

enable or even compel him to discharge his debts in a
way which is contrary to the terms of the contract and
which may in certain circumstances actually inflict
heavy losses upon his creditors.

In many cases the settlement of foreign debts
through payment into a blocked account is not compulsory, and it is left to the decision of the creditor
whether such payment should be made or not. In cases
of this kind the decision of the creditors will usually
depend upon their view of the individual solvency of
their debtors and upon their views of the likelihood of
a depreciation of the debtor's national currency. If the
debtor is of good standing, then the creditors are likely
to prefer to carry their claims in terms of a foreign
currency rather than accept payment in blocked
national currency. Even in such cases, however, it must
be borne in mind that a depreciation of the national
currency may affect the solvency of even the best
debtor if he owes large amounts in a foreign currency.
If the standing of the debtor is far from first-class, then
the foreign creditors are likely to accept payment in
national currency and run the risk of a depreciation of
that currency, or take a loss by disposing of the blocked
currency at a discount.

While from the point of view of individual debtors
and creditors payment into a blocked account may be
regarded as the settlement of a debt, from the broader
point of view of creditor and debtor countries as a
whole, such payment is no payment at all. The relation
of international indebtedness between the two countries
remains unchanged. Nor does a payment into a blocked
account reduce by one whit the resources of the debtor
country available for its internal purposes. The situation in this respect is not generally understood. Many

people are inclined to imagine that, once an amount is
paid into a blocked account, it is earmarked specifically,
and, in the same way as an earmarked gold deposit,
cannot be used for financing internal transactions.
There is in reality, however, a fundamental difference
between an earmarked gold deposit and a blocked
balance. The former is actually deducted from the gold
reserve of the Central Bank, and is, to all intents and
purposes, non-existent so far as national requirements
are concerned. The latter is, however, freely available
and can be drawn upon directly or indirectly. In some
cases the permission of the creditors is obtained for
the lending of their blocked funds for certain specific
purposes. In other cases, in the absence of such permission, indirect use is made of the blocked balances,
by granting loans which would not have been granted
but for the existence of these blocked balances. In the
case of earmarked gold deposits, it is impossible to
make use of the funds without committing a criminal
act. In the case of book entries into blocked accounts,
the boundary between the legitimate and illicit use of
the funds is not so distinct. In theory it is almost
unthinkable that a Central Bank should re-lend the
blocked funds without the consent of their owners. In
practice there is nothing to prevent it from expanding
credit to an extent corresponding to the amount of the
blocked accounts. To all intents and purposes, therefore, the amounts paid into blocked accounts are available for expenditure by the Government or by private
borrowers.

Once this fact is realised it is obvious that the
blocked currency system can easily be used for dis-
guising the insolvency of the debtors, and especially of
one particular debtor—the Government of the debtor

country. If a Government is unable or unwilling to pay its foreign debts even in national currency—apart altogether from any transfer difficulties—then, in order to conceal its default, it may adopt the practice of paying the amounts due into blocked accounts in national currency, and re-borrowing the amounts thus paid in by inducing the Central Bank or the bank in charge of the blocked account to take up Treasury bills to a corresponding amount. It is important to realise that the security provided by the system to the creditors is very slender indeed. The belief that, once the transfer difficulties have ceased to exist, the creditors can recover their blocked balances immediately, is sheer illusion. In order to be able to release the blocked balances, the debtor country has to be in a position to recover the funds lent directly or indirectly out of the blocked resources. And it is certain that the restrictions on transfers will not be removed until this preliminary condition has been fulfilled.

It is not at all surprising that most holders of blocked accounts are prepared to sell their claims at a loss. An international market has developed in every kind of blocked currencies, which are actively dealt in, either with or without the approval of the authorities of the debtor countries. The price at which the blocked currencies can be disposed of depends upon the extent to which they can be used either for payment for exports or for internal trade or investment. It is easy to find buyers for a blocked currency which can be used by importers of goods from the debtor country; it is almost impossible to find buyers at reasonable rates for a blocked currency which can only be used for long-term investments of an undesirable type in the debtor country, or for the purchase of goods which, in the normal course, could not be marketed abroad. These are the so-called "additional exports". They usually involve loss for the exporters, which has to be borne by the seller of the blocked currency, who receives a less favourable rate of exchange. Such transactions are carried out often with the knowledge and approval of the authorities of the debtor countries, who endeavour by such means to stimulate exports. Blocked currencies are also dealt in on the "black bourse" of the debtor country, while abroad they usually have a regular market. There are an immense variety of factors which determine the price of the various types of blocked currencies. In addition to the factors affecting the foreign exchanges—in themselves complicated enough these days—the blocked currencies are influenced by particular sets of considerations on their own account.

From an economic point of view the system of blocked accounts raises some interesting problems. Economists in the countries where such accounts are in operation are divided into two schools. According to the one, inasmuch as the funds held on blocked account are not used by the debtor country, the result is the sterilisation of part of its financial resources, which produces a deflationary effect. According to the other school, inasmuch as the blocked accounts are used for lending or investment, it produces duplication of credit and has decidedly an inflationary effect. In reality the effect of blocked accounts largely depends on the circumstances through which they were created and in which they are used. But for the transfer moratorium the Central Bank of the debtor country would have lost an amount of gold or foreign exchange corresponding to the total of blocked accounts. As the gold and foreign exchange reserve serves as a basis for currency and credit of a several times larger amount, the transfer moratorium in itself prevented deflation which would otherwise have taken place. Even if the amounts on blocked account are completely sterilised, the deflation involved is much more moderate than it would have been had a corresponding amount been transferred abroad. In so far as the blocked accounts are held by banks other than Central Banks the amounts involved are not sterilised, for banks have to reinvest them in some form. In so far as they are held by Central Banks the amounts involved may or may not be sterilised, according to the way in which the Central Bank treats them. As we pointed out above, in the majority of cases the funds on blocked account are employed, whether directly or indirectly.

Germany is the most important country which has introduced the blocked currency system. As a result of the various Standstill Agreements, fairly substantial blocked balances have accumulated with the Gold Discount Bank, which institute was placed in charge of blocked accounts. As is well known, the Gold Discount Bank has played an active part in the support given by the German authorities to various banks; it is impossible to ascertain how far the blocked balances have been used for that purpose. When in June 1933 the Standstill creditors were forced to agree to the postponement of the transfer of some RM.72,000,000 of blocked balances which were due to be transferred during the second half of 1933, this arrangement relieved the Reichsbank of a corresponding drain on its gold resources, and, at the same time, it enabled Germany to use that amount internally. Similarly, the transfer moratorium on the service of the long-term debt served a twofold purpose.

K

The following are the main categories of blocked marks:

(1) Registered marks, arising out of repayments under the Standstill Agreement of 1933.

(2) Credit marks, including a number of varying kinds of blocked marks, originating through repayments of credits outside the Standstill Agreement, proceeds of import balances in existence before July 16, 1931, etc.

(3) Security marks, originating through the sale of securities repatriated to Germany.

(4) Scrips issued by the *Konversionskasse* in payment of a certain percentage of the interest on long-term loans.

As a general principle, registered marks can only be used for the expenditure of foreign tourists in Germany. Elaborate precautionary measures have been taken in order to prevent the abuse of these facilities, which can only benefit those who actually spend a certain period in Germany. To some extent, however, the German authorities allow the use of registered marks for the purpose of paying for so-called "additional" exports. The meaning of this term is that goods, which in the ordinary course cannot be sold at a profit abroad, can be exported, thanks to the lower exchange rate of the blocked marks. The credit marks are used for such purposes to a greater extent than the registered marks. As a general rule security marks cannot be used for additional exports, but only for the acquisition of German securities and for certain other types of internal investment. In practice, however, the rules are rather elastic, and in some cases the German authorities are known to have granted permits for the use of security marks for the purpose of additional exports.

In order to obtain permission to make payments in these types of marks it is necessary for the foreign would-be importer of German goods to make a statement to the effect that the same class of merchandise can be obtained outside Germany cheaper than in Germany, and the German exporter has to make a statement to the effect that he is unable to reduce his prices further. The application for permits has to be passed first by the Ministry of National Economy and then by the Exchange Control authorities. The scrips are bought at a fixed price by bankers acting as agents for the Gold Discount Bank. At first they were bought at a discount of 50 per cent, but subsequently a more favourable price was fixed. The working of the system is evidently cumbersome and complicates foreign trade relations. It is nevertheless an important means of stimulating German exports. As a rule registered marks and credit marks are quoted at between 20 per cent and 40 per cent discount, while security marks are at a discount of over 50 per cent. This compares with a depreciation of about 35 per cent for sterling. Although the registered marks and credit marks are still at a premium as compared with sterling, considering the relation between the internal price-levels in Germany and Great Britain, German exporters are in many cases at an advantage. For internal prices in Germany are determined, not by the rate of blocked marks, but primarily by the official rate of exchange.

Another advantage Germany obtains through the system of blocked marks is that the Government has thereby acquired a considerable influence over the trend of the trade balance. According to whether it grants permits with greater or less liberality, it can increase and reduce exports at will. It is true that in theory an increase in the volume of permits results in an increase in the demand for blocked marks, and this again tends to reduce the discount, as a result of which it will become less profitable to use blocked marks for financing exports. In practice, however, the authorities have an easy remedy in their hands, as they can grant permits only for the use of a cheaper category of blocked marks in order to avoid an undue appreciation of the more expensive category.

The market price of the various blocked marks depends largely upon the optimism or pessimism of holders regarding the financial prospects of Germany. The reichsmark proper, since it is maintained at par by the Reichsbank, provides no indication of the changing feelings of the market. The blocked marks would provide a much more reliable barometer but for the influence of other factors which affect them considerably. In October 1933, for instance, the trend of political developments was anything but favourable to holders, but in spite of this blocked marks appreciated considerably owing to the plethora of permits granted by the German authorities to exporters.

In addition to Germany a number of other countries have elaborated highly complicated systems of blocked currencies. In Hungary, for instance, there are some seven or eight different types of blocked pengoes. In Roumania there is the blocked leu and the free inland leu, the latter being quoted at a discount of some 20 to 25 per cent. Yugoslavia, Greece, and other countries have their various blocked currencies. Austria, on the other hand, has practically liquidated the system of blocked accounts. Thanks to the foreign loan she obtained, she was able to release a large part of it and the rest was liquidated by granting permits for the use of blocked currencies for various purposes. The regulations regarding the employment of blocked currencies are subject to very frequent changes, and it requires considerable effort for bankers to keep themselves up to date.

CHAPTER XIII

THE ECONOMICS OF EXCHANGE CLEARING

ON November 14, 1931, an agreement of a rather unusual nature was concluded between the Swiss and Hungarian Governments. It was arranged that the trade between the two countries should be financed through the intermediary of the two Central Banks, obviating the necessity for Swiss and Hungarian importers and exporters to buy and sell exchanges in connection with their dealings between each other. The agreement attracted relatively little attention even in the countries directly concerned, still much less in other countries. It was regarded by most people as "just another form of irksome exchange restriction". During 1931 several new and ingenious methods of "torture" had been invented for the benefit of international trade and finance, and the reaction of the cynical and apathetic world to this new "torture" was that one more or less mattered very little. It is doubtful whether even the originators of the scheme themselves realised the true significance of their innovation. They were in all probability unaware that they had created a new system which might become the forerunner of a new era, just as Christopher Columbus was unaware that what he discovered was a new continent, and that his discovery was to change the course of history.

The substance of the agreement was that Swiss importers of Hungarian goods had to pay the purchase

price in Swiss francs into a special account kept by the
Swiss National Bank, while Hungarian importers of
Swiss goods had to pay the purchase price in pengoes
into a special account kept by the Hungarian National
Bank; Swiss exporters to Hungary were paid out of
the amounts paid in by Swiss importers from Hungary,
while Hungarian exporters to Switzerland were paid
out of the amounts paid in by Hungarian importers
from Switzerland. In reality, the agreement was not
quite so simple; there were provisions for the repayment
of old debts and for putting balances at the disposal
of the Hungarian National Bank, as well as other
details. The substance of the agreement, which was
subsequently adopted as the formula for all Exchange
Clearing Agreements, was, however, as described
above. The exporters of both countries received no
direct payment from the importers of the other
country. Their claims were cleared out of the payments
made by the importers of their own country. No foreign
exchanges were bought or sold on either side. Foreign
trade transactions were financed through the receipt
and payment of national currency by the Central
Bank.

What was the origin of this remarkable arrangement?
The decline of the gold stock of the Hungarian National
Bank through the withdrawals of funds, and the difficulties of exporting, placed Hungary in a precarious
position in the autumn of 1931. In order to prevent a
collapse of the currency, the Government had to impose rigorous exchange restrictions. Among other
measures, it was decreed that payment for goods imported was not to be transferred abroad, but was to be
made in national currency to be paid into a blocked
account. The foreign claims arising from earlier goods

transactions became frozen, and exporters of foreign countries were faced with the alternative of either stopping their exports to Hungary or accepting frozen blocked balances in payment. There was, however, a third alternative, and Swiss common sense and business instinct was not slow in grasping it. While the proceeds of Swiss exports to Hungary were blocked, Hungarian exporters were at liberty to transfer the cash received for their goods in Switzerland. Evidently, this was an anomalous state of affairs. The solution was, however, obvious; in fact, so obvious that it is astonishing how it did not occur to everybody at the very outset, and how there are still people all over the world—and especially in this country—who have as yet failed to grasp it. As Hungary blocked the balances of Swiss nationals, the obvious thing for Switzerland to do was to block the balances of Hungarian nationals. Had this been done in the form of one-sided retaliatory measures, it would have caused much ill-feeling, and trade between the two countries would have suffered. Instead, it was arranged by mutual consent; and both countries benefited by it. Hungary was able to import Swiss goods without having to find foreign currencies in payment for them. Switzerland was able to export goods to Hungary without running the risk of receiving frozen balances in payment.

As in the normal course Hungary exports more to Switzerland than Switzerland to Hungary, it was expected that the result of the Exchange Clearing Agreement would be a balance in favour of Hungary. It was agreed that this balance should be disposed of in a way calculated to benefit both parties. Part of the balance was to be used for the repayment of frozen Swiss balances contracted prior to the conclusion of the agreement, while part of it was to be placed at the disposal of the Hungarian National Bank.

Exchange Clearing Agreements have become the subject of a lively controversy. The world gradually came to realise that it was confronted by an interesting and important innovation, and expert opinion was divided into two camps, according to whether it was in favour or against the adoption of the new system. Opposition to it in the two countries that initiated it was soon overcome. A few weeks after the conclusion of the agreement with Hungary, Switzerland reached a similar agreement with Austria; in 1932, she concluded Exchange Clearing Agreements with Yugoslavia and Bulgaria; in 1933 with Roumania, Greece, and Turkey, and in 1934 with Chile and the Argentine. As for Hungary, in addition to the agreement with Switzerland, recently renewed, she has Exchange Clearing Agreements with nine other countries, viz. France, Germany, Italy, the Belgo-Luxembourg Union, Austria, Czechoslovakia, Roumania, Bulgaria, and Turkey. A number of other countries concluded Exchange Clearing Agreements with one another. They may be divided into three groups. There were, in the first place, the countries of Central and Eastern Europe which were in a position similar to that of Hungary. They concluded agreements with each other, as well as with the second group of countries, consisting of the creditor countries of Western Europe, which were in a position more or less similar to that of Switzerland. The third group included some Latin American countries, with which the group of European creditor countries concluded agreements. At the time of writing, over sixty Exchange Clearing Agreements are in operation, and the number is increasing week after

week. Some countries, such as Turkey, adopted the
new system with enthusiasm, following deliberately
the aim of basing their entire foreign trade on such
agreements. Others were admittedly more hesitating.
The fact, however, that very few of the agreements
have been discontinued speaks for itself. Some of the
agreements concluded with Yugoslavia were, it is true,
suspended, but most of them were subsequently resumed with modified terms. Austria discontinued some
agreements which were disadvantageous to her trade,
but retained those which produced satisfactory results.

The countries of the gold group adopted the system
in relation to the weak debtor countries, though not
in relation to each other or to the countries of the
sterling and dollar blocks. These latter groups kept
aloof from the movement, with the exception of the
Argentine, which, though belonging to the sterling
group, concluded several Exchange Clearing Agreements with countries of the gold group. Thus, the
isolation of the two large groups of countries, those
with and those without Exchange Clearing Agreements, is not altogether complete.

Although the system has now been in operation for
over two and a half years, most experts have failed
to grasp its real significance. It is difficult even to get
an adequate answer to the question as to what Exchange Clearing really is. Some people simply class it
with exchange restrictions. Technically, they are
right, for the act of compelling importers to pay the
purchase price to the Central Bank instead of transferring it to their creditors undoubtedly interferes
with the freedom of foreign exchange operations.   In
spite of this, nobody maintains that, because Switzerland or France have concluded Exchange Clearing

Agreements, they have adopted exchange restrictions.
It may be claimed that, far from increasing exchange
restrictions, the Exchange Clearing Agreements provide the means for overcoming them. Exchange Control is sometimes stigmatised as barter. Undoubtedly,
on some occasions the balance that has accumulated
in favour of one or other of the contracting parties
has been cleared by a goods transaction which had the
characteristics of barter. Apart from these exceptions,
however, the goods are bought and sold for cash, and
the purchase price is disposed of freely by the sellers.
It is not the concern of the individual importers or
exporters to offset their transactions by goods transactions. It is therefore not correct to regard Exchange
Clearing as barter. Nor is it right to consider it as the
extreme manifestation of economic nationalism. On
the contrary, as we shall try to prove later, it is the
best means for combating economic nationalism.

Before going further, it is necessary to discriminate
between Exchange Clearing Agreements and goods
clearing (or compensation) agreements. The latter
constitute a form of barter arranged either directly
between individual importers and exporters or between the authorities of two countries, in order to
obviate the necessity for the buyers to procure foreign
exchange in payment for their goods. To that end, the
import of certain definite goods is offset against the
export of other definite goods. In the case of Exchange
Clearing, on the other hand, importers and exporters
of both countries are at liberty to buy and sell whatever goods they want to.

There are three kinds of Exchange Clearing systems
in operation: unilateral, bilateral, and three-cornered.
The unilateral Exchange Clearing constitutes a measure

of reprisal against a defaulting debtor country by its creditor country. The bilateral Exchange Clearing is the result of an agreement between two countries, by which clearing is applied reciprocally, and the authorities of both countries co-operate with each other to enforce the clearing. The three-cornered Exchange Clearing is a highly advanced form of the system, by which the adverse balance of country A in relation to B can be offset by the favourable balance of country A in relation to country C. Apart from isolated cases, three-cornered Exchange Clearing has not so far been adopted, so that, in dealing with the system as it exists, it can be safely disregarded at this stage. As unilateral Exchange Clearing usually leads to the conclusion of bilateral agreements, it is sufficient if we confine ourselves for the present to the investigation of the latter system.

The advantages of the Exchange Clearing System may be summarised as follows:

(1) It enables financially weak debtor countries to buy from each other and from financially strong countries.

(2) It enables weak and strong countries alike to sell to weak countries and to collect the purchase price.

(3) It tends to reduce obstacles to foreign trade, such as exchange restrictions, quotas, prohibitive tariffs, and import embargoes.

(4) It tends to increase foreign trade by balancing imports and exports between two countries in an upward direction.

(5) It tends to reduce dumping by making it desirable for the exporting country to import something in return for its sales abroad.

(6) It tends to discourage exchange dumping

through a depreciation race, by making it evident that the country with a depreciating currency has to export more to pay for the same amount of imports.

(7) It facilitates the payment of old external debts in the form of exports to the creditor countries.

(8) Above all, it creates a more conciliatory spirit between Governments in their international commercial relations.

The first two advantages in the above list were duly illustrated by the example of the Swiss-Hungarian agreement. As a result of that agreement the volume of trade between the two countries increased considerably. As it was simpler and easier for Hungarian importers to pay for goods from Switzerland than for those imported from countries with which Hungary had no Exchange Clearing Agreement, other things being equal, the orders were placed in Switzerland. In fact, the relative ease with which it was possible to pay for Swiss goods resulted in an increase of Hungarian purchases in Switzerland which unexpectedly turned the trade balance in favour of the latter country.

Inasmuch as the object of exchange restrictions, quotas, embargoes on imports, and prohibitive import duties is to safeguard the currency against undue depreciation through an adverse trade balance, Exchange Clearing removes the necessity for them. Of course, if they are introduced to protect home trade then the demand for their maintenance will not weaken in consequence of the adoption of Exchange Clearing Agreements. If, however, the Government had in mind solely the safeguarding of the currency and of the gold reserve, then the object is served equally well by Exchange Clearing. For an increase of imports from a country with Exchange Clearing Agreements does not cause any additional pressure on the exchange of the importing country. On the contrary, in so far as these imports take the place of those from other countries, for which the purchase of foreign currencies would have been necessary, the pressure on the exchange is relieved. Thus, if the exchange of a country is safeguarded by a number of Exchange Clearing Agreements, its Government can afford to be more liberal also towards the imports from countries with which it has no Exchange Clearing.

Apart from this, the Exchange Clearing system tends to reduce restrictions on foreign trade also as a result of the necessity for the balancing of trade between two countries. This can be best illustrated by the case of the Czechoslovak-Roumanian Exchange Clearing, which resulted in an unexpectedly large surplus in favour of the former. It was agreed that during the following period of six months, the ratio of Roumanian exports to Czechoslovak exports should be fixed at 125 to 100. To that end, the Czechoslovak authorities were prepared to increase the quotas of Roumania in certain products, and to reduce the customs duty on other products. Generally speaking, there is a fair chance that, through the working of the most-favoured-nation clause, at least some of the concessions are granted also to countries without exchange clearing.

The result of Exchange Clearing is an increase in the volume of foreign trade, because imports and exports between the two countries tend to be balanced in an upward direction. If one of the parties has an unduly large export surplus which interferes with the smooth working of the clearing, there are two ways of remedying the situation. Either the country with the surplus will export less in future, or it will be prepared to import more from the other country. Anyone who knows how anxious every country is to increase exports can have no doubt which solution is likely to be chosen in most cases. Rather than deliberately reduce its exports, the country concerned will do its utmost to increase its purchases from the other country. Admittedly, in some cases the authorities handle the Exchange Clearing Agreements in a bureaucratic spirit, and keep down exports at the level of imports. The tendency points, however, towards a more liberal interpretation of the Agreements.

At the same time, the necessity for balancing imports and exports between two countries tends to discourage dumping. However anxious both Governments may be to increase their exports, they have to bear in mind that they will have to accept an equal amount of imports. The chances are, therefore, that they will refrain from reckless methods of stimulating exports even at a loss, for fear that they may not be able to accept imports of the same amount without unfavourable consequences to their nationals.

If the Exchange Clearing system tends to discourage ordinary dumping, there is a much stronger reason why it should discourage exchange dumping and every form of currency depreciation race. The trade of a country with Exchange Clearing Agreements derives no advantage whatever from the deliberate depreciation of the currency; for, inasmuch as it leads to an increase of exports, an equal amount of imports has to be accepted in payment for the surplus. What is more, the country with the depreciated currency will have to export a larger quantity of goods in order to pay for the same quantity of imports. This is, of course, always the case whether or not there are Exchange Clearing Agreements in operation. Under the Exchange Clearing system, however, this elementary truth becomes ever so much more evident.

Exchange Clearing facilitates the payment not only of current liabilities but also the liquidation of old liabilities. If the debtor country has an export surplus in relation to its creditors, the surplus is used partly for the repayment of old debts. Usually part of the surplus is placed at the disposal of the debtor country, which will thus be able to pay debts to other creditor countries.

What is more important, in the long run, than any of the above mentioned advantages, is the improvement in the spirit of international commercial relations between countries with Exchange Clearing Agreements. Under any other system, each country endeavours to sell the other as much as possible and to buy from it as little as possible. Hence the hard bargaining and undignified haggling that characterises trade treaty negotiations. It would be idle to pretend that negotiations in connection with Exchange Clearing Agreements are always plain sailing. There are great difficulties to overcome, and the conflict of interests remains sharp. As, however, both parties realise that they have to buy in order to be paid for what they sell to the other, the negotiations are conducted in a much more conciliatory spirit than ordinary trade treaty negotiations are apt to be.

The Exchange Clearing system is the best method of teaching the Governments of all countries a much-needed lesson in order to make them realise that in the long run they cannot export unless they are prepared to import. This may sound a truism, which should be obvious to everybody of average intelligence. In our present system, however, its truth is blurred by the network of the international exchanges, trade and credits. Under the system of Exchange Clearing, the truth appears in its nakedness. It is reduced to a simple arithmetical formula which cannot possibly be misunderstood.

Let us now examine the criticisms raised against the Exchange Clearing system. They may be summarised as follows:

(1) It diverts trade into abnormal channels, as a result of the bilateral character of the system.

(2) It favours countries with an agreement at the expense of countries without an agreement.

(3) It reduces the volume of trade by levelling imports and exports in a downward direction.

(4) It results in the maximum of interference with the exchanges.

(5) It prevents the accumulation of balances, and thus maintains the balance of international indebtedness unchanged.

(6) The accumulation of unclearable balances results in the creation of additional frozen credits.

For those who believe in free trade the first objection, according to which the Exchange Clearing system diverts trade into abnormal channels, constitutes in itself an absolutely damning indictment. Rather than have "artificial" trade they prefer to have no trade at all. In their opinion, if Canadian wheat is cheaper than Hungarian, it is the duty of Switzerland to buy the former, and the fact that through the import of Hungarian wheat Swiss exporters are enabled to recover frozen claims carries no weight in their view. They refuse to realise that, were Switzerland to follow

L

their advice, she might save 5 per cent on the purchase price of wheat, but she would on balance lose 95 per cent through having to write off bad debts. Nor could they ever forgive any country which, for the sake of very obvious advantages, renounces the dubious advantages arising from three-cornered trade. It is true that the advantages of the clearing system may be a multiple of those of three-cornered trade, but, as in every other instance when the facts speak against free trade—*tant pis pour les faits*.

Those who regard matters without prejudice must realise that in many cases the choice is not between trade through Exchange Clearing and trade through normal channels, but between trade through Exchange Clearing and no trade at all. The Central Banks of financially poor countries are, not unnaturally, anxious to preserve the last remnants of their depleted gold reserves, and are far from liberal in granting permits for the requirements of importers. If, however, the imports do not interfere with their gold reserve, thanks to an Exchange Clearing Agreement, then there is no reason why they should object to them. Moreover, the extent to which trade through Exchange Clearing is unnatural is comparatively slight. It is only on rare occasions that an unclearable balance is settled by an artificial goods transaction; apart from such exceptional arrangements, goods are bought and sold normally under Exchange Clearing. It is true that Exchange Clearing sometimes diverts the flow of foreign trade into new channels, enabling certain countries to export to markets which have not hitherto been considered their "natural markets". Such advantages secured by a country in the market of another country through Exchange Clearing Agreements are, however, no more abnormal than the advantage obtained through any trade agreement.

Admittedly, Exchange Clearing places at a disadvantage countries which keep aloof from the system. They have, however, only themselves to blame if they are not prepared to conclude Exchange Clearing Agreements. In any case, as we have seen earlier in this chapter, the beneficial effect of Exchange Clearing indirectly also affects to some extent countries which do not participate in it.

The question whether the balancing of imports and exports through Exchange Clearing is likely to be in an upward or downward direction was dealt with earlier in this chapter. In the majority of cases, the working of the system has resulted in an increase of trade between the countries concerned, or at any rate it has prevented a decline which would otherwise have taken place.

Unquestionably, Exchange Clearing constitutes a very high degree of interference with exchanges. In fact, if carried to its logical conclusion, it would amount to the suppression of the foreign exchange market. From this point of view, it differs, admittedly, but little from the extreme form of exchange restrictions adopted by many countries, as a result of which the transaction of foreign exchange business becomes the monopoly of the authorities. As, however, it has none of the disadvantages of exchange restrictions, from the point of view of international trade and finance, Exchange Clearing may be regarded as a "restriction to end restrictions".

It is argued that, since the system aims at balancing exports and imports, it must prevent any country from accumulating large reserves abroad in the form of foreign investments. Indeed, in its primitive form, Exchange Clearing tends to maintain international indebtedness unchanged, unless the creditors are prepared to accept goods in payment. This, however, is an advantage rather than a disadvantage.

Lastly, the system is accused of creating additional frozen credits in the form of unclearable surpluses on the clearing accounts. In reality, the countries which have adopted the system have always found ways so far to liquidate such surpluses, either through artificial goods transactions, or through the removal of some of the obstacles to trade. In any case, the unclearable balance is usually but a fraction of the total amount of sales to the weak country, which total would become frozen but for the operation of the Exchange Clearing system.

None of the above arguments against the system appear to be convincing. The system has, unquestionably, technical flaws, and in its present form it is far from ideal. As will be seen in the next chapter, however, many of its technical imperfections have already been repaired, and many others are likely to be repaired in the course of time. There can be no question that with the establishment of Exchange Clearing a highly efficient system of exchange control has been introduced. Its significance, even in its present relatively primitive form, cannot be overrated. To give only one example, its results in the Danubian States—where it has been adopted almost universally—are far in excess of what a Danubian Economic Union on the lines suggested in 1932 could possibly have produced. For all intents and purposes, the Danubian States have actually created a kind of economic federation through the conclusion of Exchange Clearing Agree-

ments between each other. The adoption of the system
has done more to prevent a further shrinkage of inter-
Danubian trade, and in some instances even cause a
revival, than would have been possible by an all-round
reduction of customs duties by 10 and even 20 per
cent—which is about the maximum that could reasonably have been expected of an Economic Union on
the lines proposed by M. Tardieu. Nor is this Danubian
Economic Union a closed *bloc*. Those countries which
were anxious to be included in the original Danubian
scheme—Germany, France, Italy, and Greece—have
taken good care not to be left out. They have concluded
agreements with practically all the Danubian countries, thereby securing for themselves what is equivalent
to most-favoured-nation treatment. The end which
was unattainable by diplomatic discussions and con-
ferences thus bids fair to be reached by the circuitous
route of Exchange Clearing.

CHAPTER XIV

THE TECHNIQUE OF EXCHANGE CLEARING

EXCHANGE Clearing is a revolutionary innovation in the international financial and commercial system, and its rules have not yet settled down. At the time of writing the system is just about passing its initial stages of evolution, but it will be long before it will possess a set of cut-and-dried rules. There are wide discrepancies between the details of the various Exchange Clearing Agreements, but it is impossible not to recognise, in spite of these discrepancies, certain tendencies moving in definite directions. As a result of experience, the recently concluded agreements usually adopt modifications of a more or less identical nature. On the whole it may be said that the present trend points towards an increasing uniformity among the agreements. This evolution has reached a sufficiently advanced stage to enable us to ascertain certain principles which, if not followed by all agreements, are sufficiently universal to characterise the system such as it is at its present stage.

The first question to answer is what sphere Exchange Clearing Agreements cover. As a general rule they mainly aim at covering the current items of visible exports and imports. In some agreements re-exports are also included, or at any rate a small percentage of the balances is earmarked for their settlement. On the other hand there has not been one single Exchange Clearing Agreement, so far, which has provided for the inclusion of invisible exports and imports. In a number of agreements provision is made for the settlement of old debts arising from commercial transactions. Such provisions usually assume the form of fixing a certain percentage of the surplus in favour of the debtor country, which the creditor country is entitled to use for the settlement of old commercial claims. Arrangements for the settlement of financial indebtedness occur very rarely. No arrangements have ever been made for the settlement of long-term debts, or credits subject to Standstill Agreements, through Exchange Clearing.

The normal procedure of the working of Exchange Clearing Agreements is the following: The importers of the countries concerned notify their own Central Banks as to their debts arising through the purchases of goods from the other country which is party to the Clearing Agreement. Usually they are required to submit documents, and, if these are passed, they pay in the amount in question to their Central Bank in national currency. On receipt of the payment the Central Bank immediately notifies the Central Bank of the exporting country, while the latter notifies the exporters. As a general rule the exporters are paid only if there are funds available on the Clearing Account. Thus, if a Swiss merchant exports goods to Hungary the mere fact that the Hungarian importer has paid in the purchase price to a Swiss clearing account with the Hungarian National Bank does not in itself enable the Swiss exporter to collect the funds from the Swiss National Bank. The latter only pays him if an adequate amount is available on the Hungarian Clearing Account through payments made by Swiss importers of Hungarian goods. If no funds are available, the

exporters are paid in chronological order, as and when
funds come in. Occasionally Central Banks desirous of
encouraging export trade are prepared to make advances to the exporters pending the clearance of their
claims. For instance, the first German-Hungarian
agreement provided for advances to German exporters
of up to 50 per cent of their claims. The latest German-
Hungarian agreement goes further and provides for
the immediate payment to exporters by both the
Reichsbank and the Hungarian National Bank. This
arrangement is, however, exceptional, though it is to
be hoped that sooner or later it will become the general
rule.

The attitude of the authorities in charge of Exchange
Clearing towards the accumulation of a surplus is of
great importance from the point of view of the effects
of the system on the volume of international trade.
In some cases, through sheer "red tape" or excessive
timidity, the Central Banks operate the Exchange
Clearing Agreement in a way which results in a decline in foreign trade. Instead of aiming at offsetting
the balance in an upward direction, they aim at offsetting it in a downward direction. For instance, if
country A imports more from country B than the
latter does from the former, the Central Bank of
country A refuses to accept payment into the clearing account of country B until a corresponding amount
is paid in to the Central Bank of country B as a result
of exports from A to B. In consequence, the exporters
of country B will have to wait for their money, and
they will not even have the assurance that the amount
is safely paid into the Central Bank of the importing
country. Such timid interpretation of the system is,
fortunately, the exception and not the rule. Most

Central Banks are not afraid of running up a debit balance on clearing account, as they trust that the authorities of the creditor country will take steps to facilitate the clearing of the balance by the admission of larger amounts of imports from the debtor country.

A question of great importance is that of the exchange rate. Payment is always made by both parties in their respective national currencies, though sometimes the account is kept in the stronger of the two currencies by both Central Banks. This is the case in the Swiss-Turkish agreement. If payment for imports is fixed in some third currency it is payable in the national currency of the importing country usually on the basis of the official rate quoted on the day of payment. The rate of conversion between the currencies of the two contracting countries is fixed either at the mint parity or at the official rate prevailing on the day of payment or, in the case of fluctuating currencies, at an agreed parity. As a rule the parity is fixed for the whole period of the Exchange Clearing Agreement. Should either of the parties change its mint parity before the agreement expires it usually entails the cancellation of the agreement. For countries which are on a gold basis the fixing of the exchange rate at the mint parity for the purposes of the Exchange Clearing Agreement is a satisfactory solution. On the other hand, for countries which, while maintaining the fiction of the gold standard, are unable to prevent a depreciation of their currencies in the unofficial market, it is a mistake to adopt the mint parity as the basis for their Exchange Clearing Agreements. Inland prices tend to adjust themselves to the unofficial exchange rates. As a result, if the official parity is maintained as a basis for imports and exports, it means that importers are able to buy at an unduly low price, while for exporters the prices in foreign markets are too low. Consequently, there will be an increase in imports and a decrease in exports. This was the case with Austria, which concluded Exchange Clearing Agreements with France, Switzerland, Italy, etc., on the basis of the official mint parity. It was found that these agreements were disadvantageous to Austria, and the Government decided not to renew them. On the other hand, the agreements with Roumania, Greece, Turkey, etc., which were based on the actual market exchange rate, worked satisfactorily, and were renewed.

The depreciation of the exchange of a country with an adverse balance on its Exchange Clearing Accounts involves no financial loss either to the authorities in charge of the clearing or to the importers and exporters concerned. On the other hand, it affects the country with the deficit, as it has to export a larger quantity of goods in order to settle the uncleared balance.

Once a Central Bank has received payment from an importer and credits the Clearing Account, it is liable for its equivalent in the currency of the other country. Thus, if the exchange of the importing country depreciates before the exporter is repaid, this does not affect the amount to be received by him provided that the importer paid it in to his Central Bank. By this arrangement exporters are safeguarded against losses through exchange fluctuations in case of delay in the clearing of their claims.

This leads us to the question of the legal liability of importers. In this respect the practice is undergoing a fundamental change. The terms of all early Exchange Clearing Agreements provided that the

importers had discharged their liabilities the moment
they paid in the purchase price to their Central Bank.
It was not their concern as to when the exporters were
actually paid or even whether they were paid at all.
In the new agreements, on the other hand, this principle has been completely discarded. In most agreements concluded from 1933 onwards it has been stipu-
lated that importers remain liable until exporters have
been paid. This point is of particular importance, with
regard to the possibility of a breakdown of the agreement between two countries. Although most agreements contain provisions that, in such cases, the
Central Bank of the country with a favourable balance
is entitled to collect funds from exporters until all
claims of importers are met, exporters naturally prefer
to have the additional safeguard provided by the
continued liability of their debtors.

Hitherto we have all along been speaking of Central
Banks as the executive authority in Exchange Clearing
Agreements. Although in the majority of cases it is the
Central Banks which are placed in charge of Exchange
Clearing, this need not necessarily be so. In the case
of France it is not the Bank of France but an organisa-
tion created for that purpose, the *Office de la Compensation auprès de la Chambre de Commerce de Paris*,
which fulfils the rôle of Exchange Clearing authority.
In Italy it is not the Bank of Italy itself, but the
Istituto Nazionale per i Cambi con l' Estero which
operates the Exchange Clearing arrangements. In
other countries—in Switzerland, among others—the
Central Banks have endeavoured to induce their
Governments to release them from the task of operating
the Exchange Clearing, which involves an enormous
amount of clerical work. To cover the cost, Central

Banks are usually entitled to deduct a commission from the payments they make to exporters, and in some cases it is sufficiently large to enable the authorities to build up a reserve to cover risks.

The negotiation of Exchange Clearing arrangements is difficult and complicated. If the weaker country usually has a favourable trade balance in relation to the stronger country, the latter endeavours to obtain authority to use the surplus for the settlement of old debts, while the former claims that the surplus should be placed at its free disposal. Usually a compromise is reached by which part of the surplus is used for the settlement of old debts, and part of it is placed at the disposal of the exporting country. In the case of the Swiss-Roumanian agreement, for instance, 45 per cent of the amount to be collected by the Swiss National Bank from Swiss importers of Roumanian goods is to be used for payments for Swiss goods exported to Roumania since the conclusion of the new agreement ; 35 per cent is to be used for payment for Swiss goods exported to Roumania before the conclusion of the new agreement; 10 per cent is to be used for the payment of financial indebtedness, while the remaining 10 per cent is to be placed at the disposal of the National Bank of Roumania.

In the course of the negotiations the financially weaker country usually insists on stipulating that in no case will its Central Bank be called upon to make cash transfers in settlement of unclearable balances. Exchange Clearing Agreements sometimes form part of a trade treaty, but they are never concluded for the full period of trade treaties. They usually run for from three to six months subject to repeated renewals for identical periods. Occasionally mention is made in the

Exchange Clearing Agreements of the attitude the authorities are to take concerning private compensation arrangements. In some cases it is provided that if the object of those transactions is approved, the authorities are entitled to release the parties from the obligation of arranging the transaction through Exchange Clearing. Occasionally Exchange Clearing Agreements cover only part of the foreign trade between two countries, while the rest is regulated by the other existing arrangements. In some cases, certain commodities are excluded, and the importers of those commodities have to transfer the purchase price to the exporters in the ordinary way. For example, the Austrian-Hungarian Exchange Clearing Agreement excludes the Austrian purchases of wheat in Hungary, for which Austria has to pay cash, irrespective of the status of the clearing account. In other cases, Exchange Clearing is only applied for a specific list of commodities. Again, in other cases, it is applied only for imports above a fixed quota. For instance, there is an agreement between Germany and Sweden, by virtue of which the latter is entitled to export to Germany goods for which the Reichsbank does not allot foreign currencies, being in excess of the quota. These, and only these, imports are settled by means of a limited Exchange Clearing. The proceeds of the exports are paid into a special blocked account, and are cleared with the aid of the proceeds of certain German exports to Sweden.

Some agreements contain a clause whereby the agreement does not affect the existing restrictions on imports. In practice, however, those restrictions are often modified subsequently in favour of the countries whose clearing accounts show a deficit.

As a general rule payment by importers is to be made in accordance with the arrangement made with the exporters; and the authorities do not, as a rule, interfere with such arrangements. Thus, importers are at liberty to pay in instalments if their creditors agree to such a method of payment. The Swiss-Turkish agreement stipulates, however, that for articles exported to Turkey from Switzerland for current consumption, payment is to be made within three months after their arrival in Turkey, while for deliveries for installations, constructions, etc., longer delays are admissible.

In every Exchange Clearing Agreement there is a clause by which the contracting parties undertake to do their best to enforce the working of the agreement. This means that they will endeavour to prevent the agreement being evaded or its being used as a means for illegal capital export from the other country. The conclusion of an Exchange Clearing Agreement is followed by the publication of decrees in both countries, ordering their nationals importing goods from the other country to pay the proceeds to their Central Bank. The violation of this decree is usually treated in the same way as the violation of exchange restrictions. During the early period there were frequent abuses, as importers often thought it convenient to oblige their creditors by paying them cash, thereby enabling them to keep balances abroad. To that end, it was stated that the goods imported were re-exports through the exporting country, which did not come under the Exchange Clearing Agreement. Subsequently, however, closer co-operation between customs, banks, and clearing authorities made evasion increasingly difficult. Arrangement is usually made between the two Central Banks to exchange information concerning

exports from one country to the other. It is safe to
state that at present the Exchange Clearing system,
as far as it goes, is more watertight than any exchange
restrictions.

. Although the system has improved considerably
during its relatively brief period of application, there
is ample scope for further improvements. It would be
desirable for the Exchange Clearing Agreements to
cover every kind of payments between the countries
concerned. As it is, the absence of provisions for including invisible exports and imports in the Clearing
is an omission which is sometimes detrimental to the
interests of the creditor country. If, in the trade relations between countries A and B, country A has a surplus of visible exports over visible imports, which is
offset by the spendings of the nationals of country B
in country A, there is no reason why this should not
be worked through the Exchange Clearing. Otherwise
it might prove difficult to clear the export surplus
of country A. Another improvement would be an
arrangement for immediate payment to be made by
the Central Banks of the countries concerned to their
exporters. This admittedly involves a certain risk for
the authorities, but, after all, it is to their interest that
export trade should be encouraged. As it is, delay in
payment causes loss of interest to exporters, as clearing accounts bear no interest. What is more important,
if large amounts of the resources of exporters are
tied down owing to delay in the clearing they may
become unwilling, or unable, to commit themselves
any further in the country in question pending the
liquidation of the earlier transactions. This inconvenience could be overcome without unduly heavy
sacrifices on the part of the authorities. It would

indeed be worth while from the point of view of all parties concerned to arrange for the payment of a larger commission to compensate the authorities for the risk taken by paying in anticipation of receipts.

An improvement of even greater importance than the previous suggestion would be the arrangement of three-cornered clearing. The weakest point of the system as it stands is that it is bilateral, and that as things are at present it is not possible to offset the surplus of country A against country B by the surplus of country B against country C. There were, it is true, isolated instances of such arrangements. For example, the Czechoslovak-Greek Exchange Clearing Agreement resulted in an unexpectedly large surplus in favour of the former. On the other hand, Greece had a surplus as a result of the working of her clearing agreement with Germany. It was arranged that the un-cleared balance should be settled through a transfer on account of the Bank of Greece from the Reichsbank to the Czechoslovak National Bank. Should such arrangements be the rule and not the rare exception, it would silence much of the criticism directed against the system.

The efficiency of Exchange Clearing would increase considerably if a number of countries could be persuaded to establish a permanent arrangement for the clearing of the balances obtained through the working of Exchange Clearing Agreements. The first concrete suggestion in that direction was made at the Inter-Balkanic Conference of November 1933, when it was proposed to establish a Central Exchange Clearing Office for the Balkans States. If countries belonging to a geographical or economic group—such as the

Danube States—could be induced to establish such institutions it would go a longer way towards increasing trade between them than any customs union that could possibly be established in face of growing political tension and economic nationalism.

The Bank for International Settlements would be in an ideal position to assist in the development of three-cornered clearing. Through its connections with most Central Banks it would be able to act as intermediary between them and assist them in the task of offsetting unfavourable balances through three-cornered arrangements. It might even go a step further and establish international Exchange Clearing. As most Central Banks have accounts with the Bank for International Settlements, it would be easy for the latter to make the technical arrangements required for that system. There is nothing Utopian in this suggestion. It is one of the very few international schemes which are practicable even in our days.

We have seen that, although the Exchange Clearing system is technically still far from being ideal, it has improved considerably; and the chances are that it will continue to improve. Its increasing popularity is shown by the increase in the number of agreements operating and in the amount of international trade transacted through Exchange Clearing. To give a few instances, the total amount of Swiss foreign trade financed through Exchange Clearing was 69·5 million francs up to the end of 1933. Of this amount 45·9 million francs were transacted in 1933 only. Exchange Clearing increased from 23·6 millions in 1931–1932 (over thirteen months) to nearly double that amount in 1933. In Greece, the amount advanced from 1452 million drachmae in 1932 to 4660 millions in 1933.

Other countries registered similar advances. As a large number of new agreements have been concluded since the beginning of this year, it is safe to assume that 1934 will show considerable progress compared with 1933.

CHAPTER XV

GOLD POLICY

THE policy initiated by President Roosevelt in October 1933, by which he sought to influence dollar exchange and the price-level in the United States by means of changing the official buying price of gold, has been subject, ever since its initiation, to heated controversy. The merits and demerits of this policy from a general economic and financial point of view are beyond the scope of this book. We shall confine ourselves to examining its significance as a method of Exchange Control in the light of experience.

It is not generally realised that, from the point of view we are concerned with, President Roosevelt's policy was not altogether an innovation. It had forerunners both in theory and in practice. Professor Irving Fisher, among others, advocated long before the crisis the adoption of a system by which the gold value of the dollar should be subject to changes. He was not particularly concerned with the effect of this policy upon exchange rates. His main concern was to attain by it a stability of internal prices. It would, nevertheless, have resulted in fluctuation of exchanges in accordance with changes of the gold parities, unless all other countries had adopted the same policy and had changed their gold parities always in the same proportion as the United States.

In practice, the forerunners of President Roosevelt's policy were the various devices applied at one

time or another by various authorities to interfere
with the existing gold parities without making any
official changes in them. Within comparatively narrow
limits the monetary authorities of many countries
were entitled to take steps resulting in small changes in
the gold point. The Bank of France, for instance, was
at liberty to increase or reduce the net buying price
for gold by altering the mint charges. In availing
itself of this right it changed the limits to the fluctuation of the franc. In other cases, without any particular legal provisions, situations had arisen in practice
in which the attitude of Central Banks towards various
technical points connected with gold arbitrage resulted
in a change in the gold points and a corresponding
change in exchange rates. The most typical example
of such a situation was provided by the fine gold-
standard gold controversy of 1930. The Bank of
England discontinued paying out fine gold, while the
Bank of France was not prepared to accept anything
but fine gold. As a result, the gold export point
of sterling in relation to the franc underwent a decline and sterling depreciated accordingly. In all
these cases, however, the primary object of the authorities, so far as they proceeded deliberately at all, was
not to influence exchanges but to influence gold movements. It is therefore open to doubt whether the
measures concerned can be regarded as Exchange
Control.

On the other hand, President Roosevelt's gold
policy was Exchange Control beyond question. It is
true that his ultimate aim was to influence the price-
level. This object was meant to be achieved, however,
through influencing the exchange value of the dollar.
Admittedly, according to one interpretation, President

Roosevelt, and more particularly some of his advisers, hoped to control the price-level directly through changing the value of gold. Whether or not such a policy is feasible belongs to the realms of metaphysics. In practice, so far as the price level in the United States was effected at all by the gold policy pursued in 1933–1934, it was the result of the influence of that policy upon the exchanges.

By being prepared to buy and sell gold at a fixed price, the Governments of countries on a gold basis carry on Exchange Control in the broadest sense of the term, for they prevent the depreciation or appreciation of the national exchange beyond certain points. In a way President Roosevelt's gold policy is the logical outcome of the effect of the working of the gold standard upon foreign exchanges. The substance of this system, from the point of view of its effect upon the exchanges, is that instead of having fixed gold parities the country chooses to have variable gold parities. It is only the aim of Exchange Control that has changed. Instead of aiming at maintaining the exchanges relatively stable, the authorities aim at bringing about certain exchange movements. The method adopted by them is substantially the same, whether they keep the mint parities unchanged or whether they change them from time to time.

In reality, President Roosevelt did not adopt such a logical course. By fixing an official gold buying price in October 1933 he did not adopt a "gold standard" with movable parities. To that end he would have had to declare himself prepared to buy gold from no matter what source, and to sell gold to no matter what destination, at the official gold buying and selling prices. Instead, he did not fix any selling price for gold,

and his buying price was only applicable to gold produced in the United States. Had he not gone any
further he would have failed completely to control the
dollar exchange. In order to make his gold buying
price effective it was necessary for him to buy foreign
gold, whether through authorising the import of gold
by private arbitrage or through taking the initiative
and buying gold abroad. To begin with, he preferred
to choose the second alternative. The banks acting on
behalf of the American authorities sold dollars in
London, Paris, and other centres, and with the proceeds bought gold in these markets. The result was a
depreciation of the dollar in accordance with the aims
pursued by the official monetary policy.

The question is, was it the act of gold purchases,
or the act of sales of dollars which influenced the
exchanges? Inasmuch as the dollar was controlled by
the exchange operations carried out on official American account, the system of Exchange Control was
simply active intervention. Inasmuch, however, as the
fixing of the gold price and the purchases of gold in
order to make that price effective influenced exchanges,
we are confronted with a different type of Exchange
Control. It is extremely difficult to ascertain how far,
in practice, the depreciation of the dollar was due to
the direct and material influence of the purchases of
sterling and dollar in connection with the gold purchases. The amount of gold actually bought between
October and the end of January was very small. On
the other hand, the market in dollars was narrow, and
it was far from easy to find buyers. In the circumstances
official selling of dollars, even if the amounts were
moderate, was apt to cause a substantial depreciation.

At the same time, however, the psychological effect

played also a very important part. While at first the gold price fixed in Washington remained ineffective, towards the middle of November it threatened to become too effective, mainly because of the psychological exaggeration of its influence. The market became alarmed by the persistence with which the American authorities were raising the official buying price of gold. Even though the amount of their actual purchases was small, everybody was aware that they were well in a position to make their gold buying price effective at any moment by increasing their gold purchases. For this reason the dollar rate followed the gold buying price at a distance even in the absence of substantial purchases. Towards the middle of November the market went so far as to discount a further rise in the gold buying price, and for a short while the dollar became undervalued, instead of being overvalued, as compared with its gold parities. For a moment it appeared as though the authorities would lose control of the market and that they would be unable to check the avalanche which they themselves had started. In face of that danger they resorted to the means of practically suspending the upward movement of the gold buying price. When the market realised that they did not mean to continue raising the price for the time being, there was bear covering in dollars and the dollar exchange appreciated once more above the level which the gold price justified.

It thus appears that the method chosen by President Roosevelt was not very effective for controlling the dollar. Far from reducing unnecessary fluctuations, the gold policy in October and November 1933 exaggerated them considerably. In the end the only way to avoid losing control completely was to bring the policy of deliberate depreciation to a halt. It may be objected that in any case President Roosevelt's aim was to check the depreciation at the stage at which it actually was checked, so that speculation did not force him to take steps which he would not otherwise have taken. That may be so, but it does not alter the fact that his gold policy was an inadequate method of Exchange Control. Let us assume, for the sake of argument, that his original intention was gradually to depreciate the dollar to 50 cents by raising the official gold buying price gradually to $41.34 per ounce. Had he not stopped raising the buying price of gold at the end of November, the persistent depreciation of the dollar would have provoked a wholesale flight of capital from the United States and an orgy of bear speculation. As a result, the dollar would have depreciated well below 50 cents, and the country would have been exposed to the adverse consequences of wild exchange fluctuations. It is probable that, even if President Roosevelt had intended to depreciate the dollar to 50 cents, the development of the foreign exchange market towards the middle of November would have in itself been sufficient to induce him to call a halt. It is by no means impossible that this is exactly what actually happened. If so, the attempt at Exchange Control failed deplorably, as instead of controlling the exchange, President Roosevelt's policy was controlled by it.

It was not until February 1934 that the gold policy became effective. By authorising private arbitrage to import gold to the United States and sell it at the new official buying price, the American authorities attained the end which they were unable to attain during the earlier stages of their gold policy. It was

not because the gold parity was fixed temporarily
at a definite figure in February that it has become effective; it was because the freedom of gold
arbitrage was restored. Once arbitrageurs were able
to take advantage of any discrepancy between the
price of gold in the United States and abroad, the
former was bound to become effective in controlling
the dollar. For technical reasons the exchanges were
slow, it is true, in adjusting themselves to their new
parities, but their adjustment was evidently a mere
question of days or weeks. Indeed, the latest phase
of President Roosevelt's gold policy amounted to the
restoration of the gold standard, with the difference
that there was no binding undertaking to maintain
the parities of the dollar at their new figures. We
stated at the beginning of this book that the normal
working of the gold standard is in itself a form of
Exchange Control. The character of the system as a
means of controlling the exchange becomes more
evident if the parities are changed from time to time
in order to bring about a movement in exchange
rates. This form of Exchange Control is bound to be
highly effective provided that the country concerned
is able and willing to buy and sell large amounts of
gold.

The United States was not the only country to
apply Exchange Control in the form of gold purchases. To some extent, the British authorities have
also resorted to a method that may be classed in the
category of gold policy. From time to time gold available in the London market was bought by the Exchange Equalisation Account. These purchases were
made at the current market price, as it was not part
of the official policy to influence sterling by offering

a higher or a lower price for the gold. But, then, the
American authorities, when they bought gold in
London in order to make their own official gold buying
price effective, paid the London market price and not
the Washington official price. The American gold
purchases produced a psychological effect, in addition
to their material effect on the dollar exchange. The
effect of the British gold purchases on sterling was
mainly material. By retaining the imported gold
which would otherwise have been re-exported, the
British authorities indirectly brought about a selling
pressure on sterling, and prevented an unwanted
appreciation.

It is conceivable that gold policy as a means of
Exchange Control might increase in importance considerably in the near future. Should France and all
other countries suspend the gold standard it would
become impossible for the Exchange Equalisation
Fund to intervene without taking grave risks by
acquiring foreign currencies subject to depreciation.
As the suspension of the gold standard by all countries
would create a period of utter confusion and uncer-
tainty, it is unlikely that either the Exchange Equalisation Fund or the authorities of other countries
would be prepared to take such speculative risks. At
the same time they are not likely to abandon attempts
at controlling their exchanges altogether. The only
way in which they would be able to maintain control
effectively would be the adoption of the American
method of fixing the buying and selling price of gold
at a figure corresponding to the level at which they
want to keep the exchange. It is by no means certain
that the policy would be effective, for it is doubtful
whether the amount of gold available for arbitrage

would then be sufficient to counteract other factors influencing exchanges. The experiment would nevertheless be worth attempting, especially as it is the only alternative to controlling the exchange by taking speculative risks.

In conclusion, it may be said that gold policy as a means of Exchange Control is only effective if arbitrage is allowed free course; if there is an adequate amount of gold available for the purpose; and if there are adequate technical facilities for the arbitrageur. With these conditions satisfied, gold policy is unquestionably a most efficient method of Exchange Control.

CHAPTER XVI

EXCHANGE CONTROL AND FOREIGN TRADE

HITHERTO we have been dealing with the various direct methods of Exchange Control. Intervention, restrictions, Exchange Clearing, and gold policy all have a direct bearing on the foreign exchange market. Their effect, if successfully carried out, is usually immediate. In addition to these methods, the Governments have also other instruments for Exchange Control at their disposal. They are in a position to influence exchanges indirectly through measures which affect some of the factors determining exchange movements. They can achieve this end by reducing imports; or by increasing exports; or by removing certain trade transactions altogether from the sphere of the foreign exchange market; or by regulating the flow of national capital abroad. In the present chapter we are concerned with the indirect methods of Exchange Control aiming at influencing exchanges by influencing foreign trade.

The most important of these indirect methods of Exchange Control is the method of reducing imports for the sake of safeguarding the exchange. This method was already practised during the war by most belligerent countries before any other form of Exchange Control was employed. In Great Britain the McKenna Duties constituted a characteristic example of indirect Exchange Control. Most other countries went further, by prohibiting the import of certain articles which were considered superfluous. The British authorities themselves achieved the same result through the control of the allotment of shipping tonnage during the advanced stages of the war. After the war most countries removed the embargoes on luxury imports but replaced them with increased customs duties. It is of course impossible to say how far these duties aimed at the protection of home trade and how far they served as a means of Exchange Control. In many cases import duties, which were originally introduced with the sole purpose of defending the exchange, assumed later a distinctly protective character. Although the Liberal Government which introduced the McKenna Duties in 1915 had not the least intention of protecting the British motor industry and other branches affected by the measure, their Conservative successors came to regard those Duties as essentially protective. They were removed, it is true, for a brief period in 1924 by the free-trader Chancellor of the Exchequer of the first Labour Government, but were restored and retained on the return of the Conservative Government. The original purpose of these duties was almost entirely forgotten. Although they must have been to some extent helpful in the endeavour to restore sterling to its old parity and to maintain it there, this was certainly not the object of retaining the duties.

During the economic crisis a large number of countries have resorted to import restrictions as a means of Exchange Control. The example was set by the French Government, which introduced legislation as early as July 1931 to obtain power to impose additional import duties and quotas upon the goods imported from countries with a depreciated currency. This was

a remarkable example of foresight considering that it
was not until two months later that Great Britain and
other countries went off the gold standard. Here again,
it is difficult to say how far the French Government
was thinking of safeguarding the exchange and how
far it was merely anxious to safeguard home trade.
When they were first applied, the main object of
the new measures was probably to protect French
producers against competition by countries with a
depreciated currency. At that time the franc was
considered to be entirely above suspicion, and it was
not expected that the necessity for import restrictions
for the sake of safeguarding the franc would ever arise.
Later, however, the need for such indirect Exchange
Control was increasingly realised. The fact that import restrictions were applied not only to imports
from countries with a depreciated currency but also
to imports from countries on a gold basis, shows that
the object was not merely to prevent unfair competition in the home market, but to improve the trade
balance. Indeed, on the occasion of trade disputes of
France with Great Britain and other countries, it was
officially declared that the object of the system of
quotas was to enable France to maintain the gold
standard.

It may well be asked what is the difference between
the effect of direct Exchange Control, in the form of
restricting the sales of foreign currencies to importers,
and that of indirect Exchange Control in the form of
restricting imports in order to reduce the demand for
foreign currencies. The result is in practice the same.
The only difference is that in the one case the object
is approached directly and in the other it is approached
indirectly. There is, in fact, an equivalent method of

indirect Exchange Control for each direct method of
Exchange Control. The restriction of imports through
customs duties corresponds to the restriction of purchases through charging a premium on exchanges
allotted to importers. Quotas can be applied equally
well either upon the allotment of exchanges to importers or upon the actual quantities of goods admitted
for import. The indirect method of barter arrangements corresponds in a sense to the direct method of
Exchange Clearing arrangements. As for the method
of supporting a currency by stimulating exports, it
can be done directly by paying exporters a premium
on their foreign currency holdings, or indirectly by
a large variety of subsidy devices. The method of
stimulating exports through the adoption of a system
of differential currencies such as exists in Germany,
for instance, is on the border-line between direct and
indirect methods of Exchange Control. Trade treaties
can stimulate exports by obtaining the reduction of
import duties abroad, but also by securing a favourable treatment regarding the allotment of foreign
exchanges.

There is a large variety of methods by which various
Governments subsidise visible or invisible exports for
the sake of supporting the exchange. There are direct
subsidies to producers or exporters; there are subsidies
in the form of freight reduction on state railways, and
of State-subsidised shipping lines; there are exemp-
tions from taxation, etc. The subsidies granted to
shipping companies serve the double end of stimulating
the development of national shipping and protecting
the exchange. The artificial encouragement of foreign
tourist traffic also serves a similar dual aim. Frequently
it assumes the form of enabling the foreign visitor to

acquire the national currency at a particularly favourable exchange rate.

The question is how far it is possible, in the long run,
to safeguard a currency with the aid of such methods
of Exchange Control. Is it, for instance, possible to
imagine that France will be able to remain on the gold
standard, thanks to the quotas which prevent a deterioration of her trade balance in defiance of the discrepancy between price levels in France and in other
countries? Obviously Exchange Control through import restrictions or through the encouragement of
exports creates an artificial situation. It prevents the
exchange from adjusting itself to the changed economic parities, and it also prevents the price level in
the country concerned from adjusting itself to prices
abroad. By limiting its imports to the amount of its
exports, a country can undoubtedly prevent a depreciation of its exchange through the normal factor
of foreign trade influences. If such a situation is maintained, however, for a term of years, it is bound to lead
to a contraction of foreign trade and to the economic
isolation of the country concerned, unless it succeeds
in the meantime in adjusting its prices to those of
other countries. So long as the currency of a country
is over-valued it requires a constant effort to prevent
the development of the potential adverse pressure into
actual selling pressure. On the basis of past experience
it is probable that foreign capital will keep away from
the country whose currency is considered vulnerable,
and national capital will leave the country. To eliminate such adverse effects the indirect Exchange Control
has to be supplemented by deflationary measures
calculated to bring about a readjustment.

The same considerations hold good, of course, regarding every method of artificially bolstering up the exchange in face of adverse fundamental trends. The artificial nature of intervention is not, however, as obvious in the case of indirect Exchange Control as in the case of intervention, exchange restrictions, or other methods of direct Exchange Control. Many people, who would reject the idea of supporting the exchange permanently by such means, would not hesitate to advocate indirect methods of Exchange Control as a permanent means of counteracting the effects of an over-valued currency upon the trade balance. Assuming that France maintains the franc at its present parity it may take many years before the over-valuation of the franc is entirely offset, either through a fall of prices in France or through a rise in prices abroad. In such circumstances the measures of indirect Exchange Control which were introduced in defence of the franc will become permanent institutions. The situation thus created will be no less artificial than the existence of direct Exchange Control.

The same may be said to be true if, instead of controlling the exchange with the aid of import restrictions or export subsidies, the system of barter is introduced. This is, in fact, being done on a large scale by a number of countries. The author does not share the views of those who speak of it in a tone of moral indignation or treat it with contempt as a reversion to primitive methods. Trade by barter is unquestionably better than no trade at all. If nobody wants to buy Chilean nitrate or copper, Chile is unable to buy goods abroad. Her purchases of the inevitable necessities of life would bring about a disastrous depreciation of the peso. To prevent it Chili is fully justified in buying only from those countries which are prepared to accept her

N

nitrate and copper in payment for her purchases. There is nothing derogatory in such arrangements for either of the two countries. Its chief disadvantage is that, if adopted as a permanent basis for trade, it will perpetuate an abnormal state of affairs. It is, nevertheless, to be preferred to the leap in the dark involved in suddenly removing exchange restrictions while they remain in force in other countries.

CHAPTER XVII

EMBARGO ON FOREIGN LOANS

THE embargo on lending abroad has been one of the most generally adopted methods of Exchange Control during the past twenty years. Before any other methods of Exchange Control were adopted, both in Great Britain and in France the authorities placed a ban on issuing any new foreign loans. As far as France was concerned this embargo has remained in force to the present day, though its object was not always the defence of the franc. In Great Britain the embargo was raised after the war but was restored in 1924 in order to prepare for the return of sterling to its pre-war parity. At the end of 1925 it was lifted, but the next year it had to be restored again, owing to the adverse effect of labour troubles on sterling. In 1927 it was removed once more, but the foreign loan market cannot be said to have been free in the pre-war sense of the term. In 1932 the embargo was reimposed again and it has been in force ever since.

It is not generally realised that the embargo on foreign loans is a measure of Exchange Control. Its existence is not considered inconsistent with the existence of the gold standard. In this respect an embargo on foreign loans is regarded in the same way as indirect Exchange Control through import restrictions or the encouragement of exports. Possibly the reason why its function as an Exchange Control measure is apt to be overlooked is that it is often

employed for other purposes. Its object is in some cases
to prepare the market for a conversion operation. By
eliminating the competition of higher yields on new
foreign issues, the Government of the lending country
stands a better chance of converting its own debt on
favourable terms. Much more often the object of the
embargo on foreign loans is to retain national savings
for internal trade requirements. Indeed, whenever
there is a movement in a country in favour of an
embargo on foreign loans, this is usually its chief
motive. When a country is on the gold standard, the
arguments in favour of an embargo on foreign loans
as a means of retaining the national resources at
home sound reasonable enough. If the lending country
has an export surplus which is not invested abroad,
the chances are that it will be repatriated in the form
of a gold influx and this again will widen the basis
of credit, thus supplying additional capital for home
trade. If the country has an import surplus, the embargo on foreign loans prevents or reduces an outflow
of gold, thus preventing a contraction of the resources
available for home trade.

If, however, the country concerned is not on a gold
standard, then it is sheer fallacy to assume that the
imposition or removal of the embargo on lending
abroad makes the least difference to the amount of
financial resources available for home requirements.
Obviously, sterling can only be sold by a foreigner if
another foreigner is prepared to buy it. Thus, if Great
Britain lends abroad she re-borrows the amount in
the form of an increase of the balances in London
by those who bought sterling from the foreign borrowers. The process may lead to a depreciation of
sterling or, at any rate, it may prevent an apprecia-

tion of sterling which would otherwise take place. It makes, however, no difference at all from the point of view of the amount of resources available for home trade.

In several countries the official regulation of foreign loan activity existed already before the war. The authorities in France and Germany, for instance, reserved the right to veto any loan of whose object they disapproved. This right was used for securing political advantages from the borrowers. This practice was revived by France after her return to the gold standard. As she was in possession of a large gold and foreign exchange reserve, and was running a steady export surplus, she was well in a position to lend abroad, but the Government withheld its approval unless the loans were in accordance with the aims of French foreign policy.

In some cases, since the war, there was an embargo on foreign issues the proceeds of which were not spent in the lending country. Although the primary object of such restrictions was to assist home trade, it constituted, none the less, a method of indirect Exchange Control. By preventing the granting of foreign loans from causing an adverse tendency in the value of the national currency, the authorities of the lending country interfered with the normal tendencies affecting the exchanges—which is the criterion of Exchange Control. In some cases it was the declared object of the embargo to defend the exchange, though the protection of trade was also a subsidiary motive. In 1925 and 1931 the British authorities chose to defend sterling from time to time by restricting the issue of foreign loans, instead of employing the orthodox method of raising the bank rate, because they wanted to avoid penalising home trade by an excessively high bank rate.

While the embargo on lending abroad is a positive measure of Exchange Control, it has its equivalent among the negative measures of Exchange Control. If a country is desirous of preventing an unwanted appreciation of its currency it can do so to some extent by placing an embargo on borrowing abroad. This has been done in several instances since the war. Among others, the German authorities considered it necessary, in 1927–28, to stem the flood of foreign loans. In Italy the issue of a loan abroad required the permission of the Government. In neither of these cases, however, was the object of the embargo to prevent an appreciation of the exchange. It aimed at preventing the contraction of an excessive indebtedness. Its bearing upon exchanges was, therefore, rather remote.

There are various degrees of embargo on foreign loans. In its most frequently employed form, it is an embargo on public issues. As the easiest method of raising really large amounts is by public issues, it is natural that any attempt at checking lending abroad would start with that category of loans. Until 1932 the embargo on public issues was applied, as a rule, only to flotations on foreign account. Since 1932, however, the British authorities began to apply it also to issues for British companies operating abroad.

As we pointed out in an earlier chapter, the embargo on foreign issues is, in itself, a highly inadequate method of Exchange Control. There are many ways of circumventing it by placing loans and blocks of securities privately, instead of offering them for subscription. As a result of the development of an extensive class of large investors such as insurance com-

panies, investment trusts, etc., it is now possible to
place privately loans or shares amounting to several
millions of pounds. While the resources of the small
investors are only available as a rule for public issues,
a large amount can be lent abroad without making
any offer for public subscription. This was duly realised
by the British authorities in 1932, when they extended
the embargo also to certain types of transactions which
do not involve public issue.

Notwithstanding this, the system is still far from
watertight. There is nothing to prevent investors from
buying securities in other countries. This is being
done, in fact, on a large and increasing scale. To-day
it is just as simple a matter for a small investor to buy
securities quoted in Wall Street as it is to buy securities quoted on the London Stock Exchange. While
the amount of their individual purchases is moderate,
the total involved may run into big figures. This is
a loophole the existence of which largely reduces the
value of the embargo as a means of Exchange Control.

Lastly, there is another loophole through which
capital can find its way abroad in spite of the embargo,
and that is through the granting of short-term credits.
This forms part of normal banking activity and nothing
has been done in Great Britain to interfere with it. In
other countries, such as France, Italy, and the United
States, the granting of bank credits abroad has at
times been subject to official or unofficial restrictions.
This is connected with exchange restrictions and, as
such, it belongs to the category of direct Exchange
Control dealt with in earlier chapters. It is only when
it comes to the funding of short-term credits that we
are confronted with a case of indirect Exchange Control in the form of an embargo on such operations.

On the whole it may be said that the results of embargoes on foreign loans have been far from satisfactory. The authorities can only depend on it as a means of Exchange Control during periods when the trade balance is favourable and when adverse pressure through other influences is not too strong. Apart from that, it is only helpful as an auxiliary means to supplement other methods of Exchange Control.

CHAPTER XVIII

THE FUTURE OF EXCHANGE CONTROL

HITHERTO we have been examining the various methods of Exchange Control as they existed in the past and as they exist at present. In conclusion, let us now examine the possibilities of the future development of Exchange Control. In doing so we have to discriminate between the short and long view. There seems to be little doubt that, in the course of the next few years, we shall witness a gradual relaxation of Exchange Control. But it is possible that, before we reach that stage, we shall witness an increase in the application of various forms of Exchange Control. This will be the case especially if the countries of the gold group abandon the gold standard. The result of such a change would be a geographical extension of Exchange Control; it would then be adopted by countries which have hitherto kept aloof from it almost completely. At the same time, there would also be an increase in the intensity of Exchange Control. The depreciation of currencies which have hitherto remained stable during the crisis would complicate the international monetary and commercial situation, and would lead to the reinforcement of the various measures of Exchange Control in countries where such measures already exist.

Should the countries of the gold group, on the other hand, succeed in maintaining the stability of their exchanges, the chances are that in the course of the next few years Exchange Control will decline both in extension and intensity. This assumes, of course, that during this period there will be no grave political troubles, either international or internal. A war, or even the threat of an imminent war, would be sufficient to induce the countries concerned to reinforce exchange restrictions or, at any rate, to retain the existing measures. Violent political changes within the various countries, especially if accompanied by bold economic and social experiments, would also check the tendency towards the relaxation of Exchange Control, and might even reverse the movement. Barring these possibilities, the chances are that in three or four years' time the extent of Exchange Control will be much less all over the world than it is to-day. Possibly in individual instances, such as in the case of measures taken against defaulting debtor countries, Exchange Control will be reinforced. The general tendency over a period of years, however, is likely to be a decline of Exchange Control. In most countries business interests and public opinion are longing to return to the freedom of exchanges, and they will not fail to influence the Governments to proceed in that direction.

Notwithstanding this, it would be idle to expect the abolition of all measures of Exchange Control overnight, or their complete abolition even over a longer period. Certain types of exchange restrictions will undoubtedly be removed at the earliest possible moment. It is conceivable that their removal might be hastened by international agreements to that end. There can, however, be no question of abolishing all measures of Exchange Control without discrimination.

It is probable that the measures resulting in the creation and maintenance of blocked accounts will

be the first to go. They are the most irksome of all
measures of Exchange Control, and all debtor countries should concentrate their efforts upon abolishing
them. In fact, such efforts are already being made
by various countries which endeavour to prevent the
accumulation of fresh blocked balances and to liquidate
the existing ones. Austria, for instance, has succeeded
in liquidating her blocked accounts almost completely,
thanks to the loans she succeeded in obtaining abroad
and to the moderate improvement of her economic
situation. There are two ways of liquidating blocked
balances. It can be done through adopting a liberal
attitude towards the employment of such balances.
This is being done in the case of Hungary and Yugoslavia, which countries have made some progress towards the desired end. The alternative is to consolidate
the blocked balances either by inducing their owners
to accept long-term securities in return, or through
issuing long-term loans with the aid of which the
balances can be consolidated. Several countries—Germany among others—have made offers to the holders
of blocked balances to convert them into long-term
investment, but the extent to which the creditors have
availed themselves of these offers has not, as a rule,
been very great. The efforts of the Latin-American
countries, especially the Argentine, on the other
hand, have been more successful, and their consolidation arrangements have disposed of a large part of
the existing frozen balances. The success of such
consolidation schemes necessitates the whole-hearted
co-operation of holders and creditors, and presupposes
the return of a certain degree of confidence.

The next move towards the relaxation of Exchange
Control should be, and probably will be, the adjust-

ment of official exchange rates to market rates corresponding to realities. The existence of dual exchange quotations is highly inconvenient and its elimination should be the urgent task of Governments. In the case of Austria the rates prevailing in the unofficial market have been adopted as the valid quotations for the schilling. Needless to say, so long as exchange restrictions are maintained, the chances are that there will be a difference between the rates for legal and illegal transactions. The authorities have to endeavour to reduce this difference to a minimum. Yet another step towards freedom is the termination of the foreign exchange monopoly established in a number of countries. In Roumania and several other countries, the central bank has relaxed its monopoly of exchange dealing, and authorised a number of banks to deal on its behalf, on a commission basis. In this case the abolition of monopoly has been more technical than real, as the banks authorised to deal have continued to act only as agents for the central bank. It is probable that in the course of the next few years most countries where foreign exchange monopoly exists will restore a certain degree of freedom of dealings.

It is more than probable that the restrictions directed against capital export, speculation, and luxury imports will remain in force in many countries for some time to come. Their abolition must necessarily be a gradual process, which will keep step with the general economic recovery. It is only through the resumption of international lending that the process of removing all exchange restrictions could be materially expedited. As it will be a long time before the creditor countries will be prepared to resume lending to countries whose records during the crisis were unsatisfactory, it would be unduly optimistic to expect such an acceleration of the process.

Exchange Control in the form of gold policy may be applied to an increasing degree in case of fresh currency fluctuations, but after the *de facto* stabilisation of currencies it will cease to have any particular significance. It is conceivable, though not very probable, that the United States and other countries might adopt a system of elastic currency, the parities of which would be subject to changes. In that case gold policy will become an integral part of the currency system of the countries concerned.

The removal of indirect Exchange Control in the form of import restrictions or export bounties will be slow and incomplete. It is unlikely that we shall witness the return of the same degree of freedom in international trade as existed before the war, or even during the period of post-war stability. Possibly the import restrictions which were originally established in defence of the exchanges will be retained as measures to protect home trade, in which case they will cease to constitute Exchange Control. Artificial stimulation of export trade is also likely to remain in existence, though its primary object will no longer be the support of the exchange but the support of trade. International barter arrangements will not disappear as quickly as many people expect, but in their primitive form they will have to go. On the other hand the embargo on foreign issues is likely to remain in force for some time and will probably never be abolished altogether in any of the creditor countries. It will assume the form of controlled and discriminative lending.

If there is one form of Exchange Control which is

certain to remain, it is intervention. We have said already that intervention has come to be considered as a normal part of our monetary system. Even if the gold standard is restored in most countries within the next few years, it will not be allowed to function automatically, but will be supplemented by intervention whenever necessary. The leading countries will endeavour to accumulate and retain strong reserves for that purpose. It is more than probable that both the British Exchange Equalisation Fund and its American equivalent will remain in existence in some form after the stabilisation of sterling and dollar. Possibly intervention will once more largely assume the form of international co-operation. It would, however, be unduly optimistic to expect too much in that direction. In order not to lose touch with realities, we have to bear in mind that there is every likelihood of the international political tension remaining in existence, or even becoming aggravated from time to time during the coming years. That being the case, we have no right to rely too much upon international co-operation as a means of Exchange Control. The schemes for an international currency, or even for an international gold reserve, will have to remain for a long time in the realms of Utopia. It is also unlikely that whole-hearted and unconditional assistance will be freely forthcoming when one or another country requires it. Politics are likely to play at least as great a part, if not a greater part, than they played in the international lending operations before and during the earlier stages of the crisis.

We have seen that, while exchange restrictions, gold policy, and most indirect forms of Exchange Control are likely to be gradually reduced, and even

removed, during the next few years, official intervention and the embargo on foreign loans have come
to stay. The question which is the most difficult to
answer is whether Exchange Clearing will remain or
whether it will share the fate of exchange restrictions.
At present the tendency is still towards the increasing
adoption of that system. It is conceivable that the
removal of various other forms of Exchange Control
will take the form of their replacement by Exchange
Clearing. Indeed, the adoption of Exchange Clearing
would greatly facilitate the removal of every kind
of restriction upon trade and the exchanges. Possibly
a number of countries which have not hitherto adopted
Exchange Clearing will resort to it as a means of collecting foreign debts.

There is, indeed, a strong case for retaining Exchange Clearing as a permanent part of our economic
system. It would tend to moderate and divert into
well-regulated channels the rising tide of economic
nationalism. It is the alternative to tariff walls and
attempts at economic autarchy. It would be the best
means of overcoming the difficulties of paying and
collecting foreign debts. It would be by far the best
means of safeguarding the economic system against
fluctuations of exchanges, the danger of which will
always be present owing to the continued existence
of abnormal disturbing elements. Lastly, it is in accordance with the general tendency towards economic
planning.

It is highly probable that economic nationalism will
survive the crisis which accentuated it to an extreme
degree. The growing tension and distrust in the sphere
of international politics, together with the revival of
nationalism within many countries, points decidedly

towards endeavours to attain a higher degree of self-sufficiency and to accumulate the largest possible amount of gold reserve. Every country will endeavour to import as little as possible, to export as much as possible, and to repatriate the surplus in the form of gold. Tariff wars and dumping will become the standing rule. With the aid of Exchange Clearing all these evils could be mitigated, if not removed altogether. The working of that system would make everybody realise that it is necessary to buy in order to be able to sell. It would also make creditors realise that, in order to be able to collect foreign claims, they must accept an excess of imports. Once this is duly realised, the honest debtor will no longer have any difficulty in transferring the payment of his foreign debts. The vexing question of capacity to pay, which under the present system poisons the relations between debtors and creditors, will be reduced by Exchange Clearing to a question of simple arithmetic. Creditors will no longer have any reason to suspect their debtors, rightly or wrongly, of faking their bank returns and foreign trade returns in order to evade payment. Provided that Exchange Clearing is extended over every current and capital item in the balance of payments, it will show the exact figure of the debtors' capacity to transfer payments.

Even if most countries were to succeed in stabilising their currencies in the course of the next few years, it would be unpardonably optimistic to believe that the solution of currency problems will be final. It is more than probable that after a comparatively brief period of stability the currency chaos will return. There are too many powerful disturbing factors of a permanent nature to justify hopes to the contrary. First of all it is impossible to stabilise all currencies at their economic parities. Some of them are bound to be over-valued and others under-valued. The chances are that in the course of time those currencies which are over-valued will not be maintained at their new parities. The huge floating balances, whose transfer from one centre to another was largely responsible for the international monetary disturbances of the last few years, will remain in existence. Their owners have acquired the habit of shifting them from one country to another, either for the sake of a fractionally higher yield or to avoid a real or imaginary risk. This habit of transferring capital is likely to cause at least as much trouble in future as it has caused in the past. It can only be prevented either by exchange restrictions of draconian severity, or by the adoption of Exchange Clearing. That system would also provide an effective remedy for the repercussions of sudden and substantial economic dislocations which the coming decades are bound to witness. In addition to discrepancies between prices, wages, and the standard of living in various countries, such dislocations might be caused, nationally and internationally, by technical progress and the difference between the degree of rationalisation and planning adopted in various countries. In many cases it will be impossible under any system to prevent such changes from affecting the exchange value of the national currencies. It is not the task of Exchange Clearing to bolster up exchanges at an uneconomic level. What it can do is to minimise the shock of the changes which become inevitable.

Notwithstanding the strength of the case in favour of retaining Exchange Clearing it is possible that within the next few years we shall witness its gradual removal. Human nature being what it is, after the present régime of excessive interference with the freedom of exchanges there is bound to be a general desire for the restoration of the highest possible degree of freedom. Once the emergency which brought Exchange Clearing into existence is over, the interests which had to put up with it will not leave a stone unturned until the system is scrapped. It will be difficult for most Governments to resist the pressure in favour of discontinuing Exchange Clearing. It is, however, possible that the framework of the system will be retained in some innocuous form. Possibly the banks will be required to notify the monetary authorities of their exchange transactions, so as to enable the authorities to form a clear picture of the exchange situation. Possibly the nucleus of the system will be retained in the form of voluntary transfers through central banks. Such arrangements already existed before the crisis in a number of countries. The Reichsbank, for instance, had clearing accounts with a number of central banks, providing facilities for voluntary transfer outside the foreign exchange market.

Even if Exchange Clearing is removed completely in the near future it would be a mistake to imagine that we have seen the last of it. It is certain to be restored on the occasion of the next international crisis. And, unfortunately, we have to reckon with a recurrence of the crisis before the end of the present decade. In the absence of economic planning, trade cycles will continue to operate as before, and in the absence of adequate Exchange Control cyclical crises are bound to become aggravated by unstable currency. Instead of learning a lesson from recent experience and retaining Exchange Clearing as a safeguard against its recurrence, the world will have to be taught another lesson, possibly several lessons.

Taking a long view, there can be no doubt that Exchange Clearing is the system of the future. It is unquestionably the rational form for international transfers and sooner or later it will be adopted permanently. In order to enable it to fulfil its functions properly it will have to be made watertight by extending it over every kind of international payment. It will also have to cease to be bilateral. The adoption of international Exchange Clearing, possibly under the auspices of the Bank for International Settlements, is the only form of international monetary co-operation that is practicable even in the world of political conflicts and in an atmosphere of mutual suspicion. Possibly it will take a long time before mankind will realise that international Exchange Clearing provides a permanent ideal solution of the technical problems of exchanges, trade balances, and international indebtedness. But there can be no doubt that the trend of evolution points in that direction.

THE END

Printed in Great Britain by R. & R. CLARK, LIMITED, *Edinburgh.*

4.85 = gold pt in UK -
4.82 nat lev of futures 60 days.
___

US. Spec will sell uncovered futures, promising
to deliv. £ in 60 @ 4.85

London disc rate $\begin{array}{l} + \text{ prem on forw } £ \\ - \text{ disc on forw } £ \end{array}$ } = N Y rate

Hence 6% Lon. rate - 4% p.a. premium on forward
= NY rate of 5% — If less than 4% p.a
there is a spec. position in spot sterling.